HOLY SPIRIT

ARE WE
FLAMMABLE
OR
FIREPROOF?

Before you start reading this book, please get hold of some HIGHLIGHTERS and mark what blesses you.

May I ask you for a favor? If you have been blessed, please promise that you would recommend this book to your friends.

HOLY SPIRIT

◆

ARE WE
FLAMMABLE
OR
FIREPROOF?

REINHARD
BONNKE

Australia • Brazil • Canada • Germany • Hong Kong • Singapore
South Africa • United Kingdom • United States

© 2017 by Reinhard Bonnke
HOLY SPIRIT Are we FLAMMABLE OR FIREPROOF?

Published by Christ for all Nations
PO Box 590588
Orlando, FL 32859-0588
CfaN.org

ISBN: 978-1-933446-52-3 (paperback)
ISBN-13: 978-1-933446-53-0 (e-book)

ESPÍRITU SANTO: ¿Somos inflamables o a prueba de fuego?
ISBN: 978-1-933446-54-7 (Spanish paperback)
ISBN: 978-1-933446-55-4 (Spanish e-book)

Edited by Pastors Solomon and Michelle Ofori-Ansah
        PrimeDoor Media and Marketing PrimeDoor.org
Interior Design by Grupo Nivel Uno Inc.
Cover Design by DesignstoGo.net

Printed in China

FIERY CHARIOT!

Evangelism is a fiery chariot with a burning messenger,
preaching a blazing Gospel on wheels of fire!
Allow the Holy Spirit to make your ministry His chariot.

DEDICATION

I dedicate this book to my dear wife Anni, who
has faithfully been at my side in marriage, family
and global ministry for over 53 years.

Just last week, I said to her: "When I look
on your face, I see the rising sun."

When we started our lives together, we chose Psalm 113:3,
"From the rising of the sun, till the going down of
the same the name of the Lord be praised."

REINHARD BONNKE

TABLE OF CONTENTS

PREFACE

I was invited to preach at a Christian meeting where the people did not believe in the power of the Holy Spirit. Suddenly, in the middle of my service, the Holy Spirit fell, and the people were rejoicing, being filled with the Spirit and praising. When I looked at the crowd, right in the middle were three or four people who were totally untouched. They had their eyes open and were looking around instead of participating in the supernatural event. And then it came to my heart—these people must be *asbestos Christians*. They were fireproof, even when the fire of the Holy Spirit fell. I want to tell you, I personally am flammable for God. I want to burn with the fire of the Holy Spirit and carry a burning torch right to the end of my life. This experience gave me the title of this book. And I put that question to you today. Are you flammable or fireproof?

INTRODUCTION

The book of Acts reads better than any modern novel. It has clearly defined characters–some in leading roles and others as supporting cast. It has action, adventure, triumph and tragedy. The scenes change from Jerusalem to Damascus to Antioch to Rome, from prison cells to shipwrecks. We encounter the wind of the Holy Spirit and the emboldened peasant apostles who moved in phenomenal miracles and baffled government leaders of their day. However, these great apostles were not always distinguished nor did they always act nobly.

I was startled when I read in Mark 16:8 that the disciples, before Jesus ascended to heaven, did not believe. The same unbelief is found in Mark 16:11. Then, two verses later in verse 13, the same four words–*they did not believe*. Again, in verse 14, the same four words–*they did not believe*. They were a bunch of unbelievers! But what amazes me most is the fact that in the next verse, verse 15, Jesus said to these unbelieving and fearful believers, "Go into all the world and preach the Gospel to every creature." If I had been there, please allow me to say this, I would have approached Jesus from behind and whispered into His ear, "Master, Lord, don't You know that the disciples You just gave the Supreme Commission to are a bunch of unbelievers? They will never be able to do it." I think Jesus would have turned around, put His finger over His lips and said quietly to me, "Bonnke, you don't know that I have a secret."

What was the secret? Something happened between verse 14 and verse 20. In verse 20, we read, "They went out and preached everywhere, the Lord working with them and confirming the Word through the accompanying signs, Amen." What happened between verse 14 and verse 20? Chronologically, Acts Chapter 2 happened. The disciples walked out of weakness and arrived at the power to do what Jesus had commissioned them to execute after He ascended to heaven: "But you shall receive power after the Holy Spirit has come upon you, and you shall be witnesses to Me in Jerusalem and in all Judea and Samaria and to the end of the earth" (Acts 1:8). In the same way, we all can leave weakness and step into unending power.

Power is the essence of the Christian witness. It is not a Gospel accessory. It is not the bell on a bicycle—it is the whole machine! There is never the slightest hint that some disciples would be powerless. To be blunt, Christianity is either supernatural or nothing at all. We had—and still have—a supernatural Jesus, with a supernatural ministry, creating a supernatural Church, with a supernatural Gospel and a supernatural Bible. Take the miraculous away and you have taken Christianity's life away. The Church becomes an ethical society or a social club when it is intended to be the grid system for transmitting the power of God into this powerless world. You and I are conductors of God's power to the world!

The Holy Spirit and the Gospel of Christ's redeeming love are inseparably tied together in the bundle of life. If you want to see the power of God, then ignore all the techniques, manipulation and psycho-suggestion and simply preach the Word! That is where the power of God is released—right in the Gospel. I do not take only one thing out of God's treasure chest. I proclaim the whole Gospel, which contains everything that we human beings need—salvation, forgiveness, healing peace, hope and deliverance.

I have penned some strong teachings on the Holy Spirit for you, and I have put together some dynamic Points of Power on the Holy Spirit (FIRE POINTS). I want to challenge your thinking on the Holy Spirit and inspire you to believe in the amazing power of the Spirit within you. There is a dynamic, dead-raising power on the inside of you. God has made it available to every believer. There is no excuse for weakness against sin or evil. After all, we can do all things through Christ who strengthens us (Philippians 4:13).

To tell you the truth, this book summarizes the secrets of my life and ministry. I know for sure, if you apply these principles, they will do the same for you.

Multitudes have been baptized in the Holy Spirit during our Gospel campaigns, and we regularly witness mighty manifestations of the power and love of God. I want to explain the understanding that I have gained from these events. My final authority is always the Bible. Certainly, experience has helped me to grasp the things of the Spirit, but as Peter wrote, God "has given to us all things that pertain to life and godliness" (2 Peter 1:3). Scripture validates experience. In sharing my understanding of the things of the Spirit, I try to show that my conclusions are arrived at through the Word, illuminated by what I have seen.

RAPID GOSPEL FIRE

For I am not ashamed of the Gospel of Christ, for it
is the power of God to salvation for everyone who
believes, for the Jew first and also for the Greek.

ROMANS 1:16

TAKE THE SAFETY OFF

The Gospel is the only gun which brings a dead man back to life when shot.

FOUNDING DOCUMENTS

*The Bible is the constitution of the Kingdom of God. No majority of any parliament
on earth, no earthly government or Supreme Court can change it. Democratic vote or
consensus does not decide Bible truth. "Forever, O Lord, Your word is settled in heaven"
(Psalm 119:89). Jesus said, "I am the truth" (John 14:6).*

BREAKING NEWS

The Gospel, when preached, happens! It becomes an event.

UNLEASH THE FIRE

*We do not defend the Gospel with barbed wire. The Gospel is best defended when exposed
to its enemies. It knows how to tackle them.*

ROCK SOLID

*The Word of God is a solid rock, not a heap of pebbles which is a collection of Christian
opinions.*

AMBASSADORS

The Gospel is not an amendment to improve a human resolution. No matter how humble the Gospel preacher, effectively he is an officer of the Crown, speaking with authority from the Kingdom of God. "We are ambassadors for Christ" (2 Corinthians 5:20).

NOT MAD NEWS

The Gospel is not a word of judgment. It is GLAD news, not MAD news. Christ is the Resurrection and the Life.

ALWAYS FRESH

The Gospel is not a story which has been preserved like the story of Alexander the Great. It isn't a mummified relic of the past. There's no such thing as old electricity or old wind, and there's no such thing as an old Gospel.

AGELESS

The Word of God is as ageless as life. It is not an antique needing preservation. God preserves the church. "In Him we live and move and have our being" (Acts 17:28).

GOSPEL GRENADE

When faith and witness combine, it produces something like an explosion. Paul said the Gospel is "the power of God" (Romans 1:16).

NATIONAL SECURITY

The Gospel is nothing less than a nation-saver. It is a power pack for the nations, designed to put a dynamic charge into all life. Jesus saves!

FIRE POINTS

SECTION 1:

HOLY SPIRIT HIGHLIGHTS

GOD OF WONDERS

"Now when He (Jesus) got into a boat, His disciples followed Him. And suddenly a great tempest arose on the sea, so that the boat was covered with the waves. But He was asleep. Then His disciples came to Him and awoke Him, saying, 'Lord, save us! We are perishing!' But He said to them, 'Why are you fearful, O you of little faith?' Then He arose and rebuked the winds and the sea, and there was a great calm. So the men marveled, saying, 'Who can this be, that even the winds and the sea obey Him?'"

MATTHEW 8:23-27

MEGETHOS—UNSTOPPABLE POTENCY

> *Through the baptism of the Holy Spirit, we all have access to a dead-raising, resurrection power. A powerless church is a disgrace. The Holy Spirit is always in on the act when you act for God. If you don't work for God, you don't need power, and none will be given. But once you are baptized in the Spirit, the potency is unstoppable.*

PAUL PRAYS FOR THE EPHESIANS (1:18-20 NIV) THAT "THE EYES of your heart may be enlightened in order that you may know...His incomparable great power FOR US who believe. That power is like the working of His mighty strength, which He exerted in Christ when He raised Him from the dead." Paul uses a word here to describe the greatness of the available resources—*megethos*. The nuclear bomb is measured in "megatons." But Paul goes one better and talks about "hyper *megethos*" or super greatness. That is how we should measure our effectiveness in Christian service, and that is the resource available to every one of God's servants.

THE IMPOSSIBLE HAPPENS

> *The Divine nature is not just supernatural; it is miraculous. God's power, love and goodness transcend all matter. Where the presence of God is, expect light, life and excellence—mountains are made low, valleys are lifted and the crooked is made straight (Isaiah 40:4). There is no such word as impossible in God's dictionary.*

THE IMPOSSIBLE HAPPENS WHEN GOD IS AROUND. IT IS HIS hallmark. Creation itself began when He passed by. Job speaks of the universe as "but the outer fringe of His works" (Job 26:14 NIV), like a track left by walking on wet grass. It was the same with Jesus. You could tell when He had passed through a Jewish village. There were no sick people left! Where He is, there's no problem with walking on waves, healing the sick or feeding 5,000 with a boy's packed lunch. It just happens; the elements bend to His will. "God causes EVERYTHING to work together for the good of those who love God..." (Romans 8:28 NLT).

THE MIRACLE HOLY SPIRIT

God is not just supernatural; He is miraculous by nature, and so is His Spirit. Everything about Him is miraculous, and so is everything He does. To have the Spirit is to expect the miraculous, to believe in the Spirit is to believe in the miraculous, and to walk with the Spirit is to move and work in the miraculous. You are made for signs and wonders!

THE ONLY SPIRIT THAT JESUS PROMISED US IS THE MIRACLE Spirit—the Holy Spirit. There is no non-miracle Holy Spirit. To claim to possess the Holy Spirit and deny the very work which has always distinguished Him can only grieve Him. He began with the supreme physical wonder of creating the world. He does not change His nature. What He was, He is and always will be—God operating on the earthly scene. "I am who I am" (Exodus 3:14). The Holy Spirit, who made the world supernaturally, should have no difficulty in continuing supernaturally.

BEYOND YOUR EXPECTATIONS

> *Fallen, weak and human, our natural tendency is to doubt and rationalize the things of the Spirit, but in Christ Jesus, our spirit is reborn. Now we have faith to live in the supernatural and believe for the miraculous. Don't let your natural state or physical circumstances talk you out of your miracle.*

GOD CREATED THE NATURAL ORDER AND OPERATES through natural law. He is neither bound to nor limited by them or our weaknesses. He is able to exceed our expectations and even our wildest dreams (Ephesians 3:20). And we can trust this. After all, "God is not a human, that He should lie, and He is not a human being, that He should change His mind. Does He speak and then not act? Does He promise and not fulfill?" (Numbers 23:19 NIV).

BAPTIZED IN FIRE

"I indeed baptize you with water unto repentance,
but He Who is coming after me is mightier than
I, whose sandals I am not worthy to carry. He
will baptize you with the Holy Spirit and fire."

MATTHEW 3:11

THOROUGHLY BATHED

> *The baptism of the Spirit is a complete immersion of your entire being—spirit, soul, body—into the Holy Spirit. It is not partial, symbolic or temporary. Every part of your being is dipped and thoroughly bathed in this precious Liquid Fire, permanently. It is not a one-time event, as in water baptism. It is an ongoing experience that changes your very nature and surroundings.*

SOME PEOPLE WANT ICE CREAM CHRISTIANITY, COLD BUT nice. They want their churches to be like museums. But the church is not a freeze box. It is the Father's house. The Holy Spirit warms us up for the Father's house.

ENDUED WITH THE SPIRIT OF THE PROPHET

> *Abraham, Moses, Joshua, Deborah, Elijah and Elisha—all these names inspire awe and wonder, but they were human with passions like you and I (James 5:17). The same Spirit that was upon them is in us. We did not receive a second-rate Spirit or experience, and we should not expect a second-rate result.*

THE BAPTISM IN THE SPIRIT ENDUES BELIEVERS WITH THE Spirit of the prophets. When the prophets experienced God supernaturally, they called it the Spirit of the prophets. Joel 2:28 promised that the same Spirit of the prophets would be poured out on all flesh. People of all kinds would prophesy, not just an individual here and there.

AN ELECTRIC CABLE LOOKS TAME UNTIL IT IS TOUCHED

> *The Kingdom of God has come, and we hold the keys to it. We may look ordinary, innocuous or inconsequential, but make no mistake, we are full of power—the power of the Holy Spirit—and we are vital to God's redemptive plan. Our tongues have the power to impact destinies and change the course of events, and in our hands, we carry the healing balm of Gilead.*

WHEN ELECTRICITY WAS FIRST DISCOVERED, IT WAS considered by most observers to be an amusing novelty. Two hundred years ago, few people could conceive of the potential of the power of electricity to drive industry and light whole cities. When people speak with other tongues, it is a sign of the potential of the power of the Holy Spirit. We can derive our confidence in what God can do from the manifestation of the Spirit. The Spirit of God will not be limited to isolated incidents but will permeate our entire ministry if we let Him. Looking tame? Christians may look tame, but so does an electric cable—until you touch it.

YOU SHALL RECEIVE POWER

"Therefore, when they had come together, they asked Him, saying, 'Lord, will You at this time restore the kingdom to Israel?' And He said to them, 'It is not for you to know times or seasons which the Father has put in His own authority. But you shall receive power when the Holy Spirit has come upon you; and you shall be witnesses to Me in Jerusalem, and in all Judea and Samaria, and to the end of the earth.'"

ACTS 1:6-8

EXUBERANCE

> *Jesus said, "You shall receive power when the Holy Spirit has come upon you" (Acts 1:8). Without that vitality, we have a secularized, rationalized and harmless religion. Mystical contemplation bears no resemblance to New Testament dynamism; quietism is for Buddhists, not Christians. Don't hold back!*

HOLY SPIRIT EMPOWERMENT IS INTENDED TO BE THE NORMAL way Christians function. Being filled with the Spirit is shown to have had a dynamic and energizing effect, or "power" (*dunamis*), in the New Testament and in the lives of millions of people since then. There is very little Scripture to suggest that the Holy Spirit comes upon men like a quiet breath, unobtrusive and unnoticed. It is usually very noticeable. Manifestations of the Spirit include fire, wind, noise, wonders, outward signs, power and visible effects.

POWER TO PREVAIL

> *The Holy Spirit is not a super-drug, a tranquilizer or a stimulant. He does not come to give us an emotional experience, but make no mistake about it: His presence is heart-moving. Life is tough. God sends His power to people in tough situations. He is the original life force meant to empower us to live victoriously, abundantly and to be a witness to the world.*

"YOU SHALL BE BAPTIZED WITH THE HOLY SPIRIT NOT MANY days from now...You shall receive power when the Holy Spirit has come upon you" (Acts 1:5, 8). Could it happen in our time? Well, it did for me. I cannot think of anything more wonderful for human beings than that. It means being filled with God. It is not 'getting high' on God, a sort of euphoric, giddy happiness, all froth and bubble. It is about real enablement, strength of character, healing in the body, Divine protection, wisdom, and an increase in intelligence, favor, and all the goodness we need to live this life.

POWER FOR THE MARATHON

Precious as it is, you don't earn the anointing like an elite athlete receives an Olympic Gold medal. Like our salvation, we receive the Spirit by faith, not because we are worthy or deserve it, but to empower us to be a witness for Christ.

THE POWER OF THE HOLY SPIRIT DOES NOT COME AS A reward. Power is not a trophy at the end of a marathon. We need power at the start if we are to run the marathon for God. We may be disgraceful, perhaps stumbling in our walk, but that makes it so necessary for us to receive the Holy Spirit. He is not given on condition that we are perfect. He is given because we are not perfect. He has come because we need Him—for the best and for the worst of us. Just repeat in your heart: "Holy Spirit, I really need you!" His response is immediate—He is there.

EVER PRESENT HELP

"And I will pray the Father, and He
will give you another Helper, that He
may abide with you forever."

JOHN 14:16

THE OMNIPOTENT HOLY SPIRIT WORKS THROUGH US

> *The Holy Spirit is the Spirit of God—the Spirit of Jesus Christ. He is God. We do not reinforce the Holy Spirit by prayer—He is omnipotent without our help. Nevertheless, Scripture says that we should pray in the Spirit (Ephesians 6:18).*

THE HOLY SPIRIT IS GOD, THE THIRD PERSON OF THE TRINITY. He is omnipotent, omniscient and omnipresent. He does not need our help, but He chooses to use us—to work with us, through us and for us—out of love. Prayer is not helping God; it is helping us partner with God, surrendering to Him and allowing Him to take His place as Lord of our lives—Deliverer and Savior. What an honor bestowed on us that we should be graced with such prestige as to be agents of a good, holy and gracious God! In a world filled with pain and suffering, we offer salvation.

GOD WANTS TO WORK FOR YOU

> *Many are working for God, when God wants to work for them. He doesn't want us to work so hard that we drop dead for Him. The work of the ministry is vital, even critical, and it is time sensitive. However, God still wants us to find time to rest and be with family and friends, enjoying the good things freely bestowed on us.*

I SAW A GRAVESTONE ONCE WITH A MAN'S NAME AND epitaph: "His life only consisted of work." I mused, "That is an epitaph for a mule and not a man." God didn't intend for us to be beasts of burden or to labor like robots. He could create pack horses in abundance, if that's what He wanted. But when the Lord thought of you and me, He had something in mind other than slaves—sons, not trams.

DON'T LIMIT HIM

"How often they provoked Him in the wilderness,
and grieved Him in the desert! Yes, again
and again they tempted God, and limited the
Holy One of Israel. They did not remember
His power: The day when He redeemed them
from the enemy, when He worked His signs in
Egypt, and His wonders in the field of Zoan."

PSALM 78:40-43

NO SUBSTITUTE

> *The Holy Spirit has no substitute. He is the life in the preacher and the power in the sermon, the divine magnet that attracts souls to the Church. The Spirit of God is His own advertiser; if we will let Him take His place in the Church and build it, the gates of hell will not prevail against it. We will see growth.*

THE LESS HOLY SPIRIT OPERATION WE HAVE, THE MORE CAKE and coffee we need to keep the church going. Nothing against coffee or cake, but the truth remains that the Holy Spirit has no substitute. His presence and works speak for themselves.

THE WHOLE WORLD FOR JESUS

> *The Holy Spirit makes evangelism possible. Without the Holy Spirit, the Great Commission is only an impossible dream. But with the impetus and involvement of the Holy Spirit, preaching the Gospel to all creation is not just wishful thinking. It is an attainable vision.*

AT THE BEGINNING OF THE LAST CENTURY, HOLY SPIRIT manifestations dramatically increased just like in Acts 2. From America, it spread to Europe, to Asia and across the world. My question is, if in the last 100 years, 20 people on fire for God could bring 800 million souls to salvation, how many will those 800 million bring to salvation now? Not even the sky is the limit with God!

"I SEE JESUS IN YOUR EYES"

The Holy Spirit has taken residence in you and wants to move in your life with power. He wants to connect with every member of your being and with every faculty of your soul. Surrender—your tongue, your body, your mind, your will and even your eyes—and people will see Him in you.

YEARS AGO, MY MUSIC MINISTER AND I WERE SHOPPING FOR a new keyboard. It was noon as we entered a big music shop in Johannesburg, South Africa. The salesman took no notice of us as we tried out all the keyboards. Suddenly, the salesman appeared. He seemed to be in a state of shock as he said to me, with eyes wide open, "Sir, I can see Jesus in your eyes!" What? The Holy Spirit had entered that shop. We forgot all about the keyboard and had a revival instead. But when I was walking back to my car, I kept saying, "Lord, I will never understand. How can a total stranger walk up to me and say, 'I can see Jesus in your eyes?'" Suddenly, the Holy Spirit spoke to me and said, "Jesus lives in your heart, and sometimes HE LIKES TO LOOK OUT OF THE WINDOWS." I laughed and cried. What glorious truth! I got the point. Years later, I met the wife of the salesman who told me that her husband had followed Jesus for the rest of his life. Praise God.

ALL OUT FOR JESUS

"Therefore we also, since we are surrounded by so great a cloud of witnesses, let us lay aside every weight, and the sin which so easily ensnares us, and let us run with endurance the race that is set before us, looking unto Jesus, the Author and Finisher of our faith, Who for the joy that was set before Him endured the cross, despising the shame, and has sat down at the right hand of the throne of God."

HEBREWS 12:1-3

PUBLIC NOT PRIVATE

*Are we ashamed of the Gospel? Paul wasn't. He shaved his head to show
that he had made a vow (Acts 21:24). People would notice that—a skinhead
apostle. But HE WAS NOT ASHAMED! He had sworn an oath to do
something for God! Why not we fire-baptized believers?*

WHEN THE 120 EMERGED FROM THE UPPER ROOM, THEY
were different! They were sealed, changed and that change was
noticeable. What do people look like who emerge from our churches
on a Sunday morning? Suppose God's fire fell in a stadium during a
Gospel crusade and everybody came out drunk with the Holy Spirit?
The baptism in the Holy Spirit is NOT A PRIVATE MATTER! It is a
PUBLIC EVENT! Glory to God!

FULL THROTTLE

*The world admires every passionate enthusiasm except one: love for God.
What do we want? Do we want our cozy culture and sophistication—or the
burning and throbbing drive of the Divine nature? If you want all of Him,
then you have to go full throttle.*

THE GLORIOUS EXPERIENCE OF BEING SWEPT INTO THE
ocean of God's purposes, carried along in that Pentecostal mighty
rushing wind—is that what we are afraid of? Has the starch of what
we call civilization stiffened our clothing and turned it into steel
armor so that it has become difficult to 'put on Christ?' Where
are His tears? His passion—our cross—bearing? Where is our total

unselfconsciousness and yieldedness to God? If you want all of Him, then you must go full throttle. Don't hold back.

WHERE TO BEGIN

> *A young man told me that he had a call to preach the Gospel, but his pastor was not willing to give him his pulpit. I looked at him and said, "I will give you a pulpit!" He looked at me wide-eyed and said, "What? You want to give me your pulpit?" I said, "No, but I can give you a pulpit. Every street corner is a pulpit." I continued, "That is where I started, and you have to begin there as well." The Scripture says, "Do not despise these small beginnings, for the Lord rejoices to see the work begin" (Zechariah 4:10 NLT).*

MINISTRY GROWTH COMES IN PHASES. GROWTH HAPPENS slowly. You will mature in the Word, in faith, in the Holy Spirit and in bearing fruit. Don't give up when opposition comes. Jesus made us more than conquerors. We have an open heaven, angels ascending and descending, our prayers reaching heaven unhindered, and the Holy Spirit constantly pouring upon us like sunshine from a cloudless sky.

FIRE POINTS

THE SPIRIT AND THE SON– JESUS THE BAPTIZER

THE ANOINTED ONE

"When He had been baptized, Jesus came up immediately from the water; and behold, the heavens were opened to Him, and He saw the Spirit of God descending like a dove and alighting upon Him. And suddenly a voice came from heaven, saying, 'This is My beloved Son, in Whom I am well pleased.'"

MATTHEW 3:16, 17

BAPTISM IN FIRE

Jesus said that John the Baptist was a burning and a shining lamp, but he baptized with water in the cold waters of the Jordan. But Jesus is not a lamp. He is the Light, the Lord Himself. He baptizes in a different Jordan, the spiritual one, which is blazing hot with fire from the altar of God, bringing healing and power.

JOHN THE BAPTIST KNEW ABOUT BAPTISM IN THE SPIRIT, FOR God told him. In fact, John said that is how we would identify Christ. Baptism in fire would distinguish Him. It would be something that nobody else had ever done or ever would do. There are religions a-plenty, but Christ stands apart. Only He baptizes in the Holy Spirit and fire (Matthew 3:11).

JESUS WAS BAPTIZED IN THE HOLY SPIRIT

Though conceived by the Holy Spirit, Jesus needed the baptism of the Spirit as He embarked on His ministry. As John the Baptist baptized Jesus in the Jordan, a second baptism took place. The Spirit of God descended on Him, like a dove, not as a flame of fire, because there was nothing to burn in Jesus.

THE GREAT PATTERN FOR CHRISTIANS IS JESUS, AND HE WAS baptized in the Holy Spirit. The Gospels of Matthew, Mark and Luke all record the same event. The fourth Gospel, John, gives more detail. John the Baptist, the fore-runner of Jesus, declared, "I saw the

Spirit descending from heaven like a dove, and He remained on Him" (John 1:32). Jesus Himself explained, "The Spirit of the Lord is upon Me, because He has anointed Me to preach the Gospel..." (Luke 4:18). Peter, in Acts 10:38, said, "God anointed Jesus of Nazareth with the Holy Spirit and with power." John the Baptist said a thrilling thing. "He who sent me to baptize with water said to me, 'Upon Whom you see the Spirit descending and remaining on Him, this is He who baptizes with the Holy Spirit'" (John 1:33).

Christ had a human experience from God to show what the perfect human experience should be. He was the first of multitudes. He was the first Holy Spirit-baptized man on earth. John 3:34 (NIV) says, "God gives the Spirit without limit." John 1:16 declares, "Of His fullness have we all received..." That is the wonderful truth—what He received was for us. He was filled for us, and out of His infinite fullness we are filled.

EVERYTHING JESUS DID WAS FOR US

He was born for us, and He lived for us. He said that He was baptized in water and in the Spirit for us. He ministered, died, rose, ascended to glory and is coming back for us.

THE HOLY SPIRIT TRANSLATES JESUS' LIFE INTO OUR experience. When He chose the role of human, He accepted humanity's need for the Holy Spirit. He identified Himself with us, and said, "Thus it is fitting for US to fulfill all righteousness" (Matthew 3:15). Jesus was the Son of God, but He stood where we all stand as human beings. This meant that the day came when He moved into a new experience, endowed with the Spirit. It was not conversion or new birth. The Son of God never had that need. His example showed that the baptism in the Spirit is not to be confused with regeneration or any other spiritual event. He received a separate and unique experience of the

Holy Spirit for His ministry. That is how it should be for us all, as we follow His example.

ANOINTED TRACKS

These are the giant footprints of a man or woman bathed in the liquid fire of the Holy Spirit. Every step drips with fire that scorches scorpions and serpents in our path, leaving a trail of deliverance and blessings.

THE WORD "BAPTISM" IS TODAY A CHURCH-RELATED WORD, but in ancient times it just meant immersion. When a dyer put cloth into dye, it was immersed or baptized, meaning that the fabric took on the nature of the dye. When Jesus, standing in the river of the Holy Spirit, calls us and we follow, He puts His arm around us and baptizes us in the liquid fire of the Holy Spirit. We are then in the fire, and the fire is in us. As we rise from this glorious river, we realize that we are completely saturated and totally soaked. This is not for one aspect or function, but represents the immersion of our entire personality. Imagine you get out of the river, and you feel how this living fire drips from you. Every devil in town will know where you went, because they can recognize the drops of fire in your footprints. Anointed tracks!

BEING INCLUDED

Jesus did not baptize anyone with fire during His earthly life. He said that He would do it after He had gone to His Father. And He did, beginning with the Day of Pentecost recorded in Acts 2. That 'afterward' is still going on. There's no change of program. Jesus is still the Baptizer in the Holy Spirit. He has not retired or changed His role. How could He, when the promise is for people "afar off?" (Acts 2:39).

A NEW CHAPTER OF THE ACTS OF THE APOSTLES IS BEING written. Today, the baptism in the Spirit inspires hundreds of millions of new believers in power-evangelism. Be included!

THE SON'S PASSION

"When it was almost time for the Jewish Passover, Jesus went up to Jerusalem. In the temple courts, He found people selling cattle, sheep and doves, and others sitting at tables exchanging money. So He made a whip out of cords, and drove all from the temple courts, both sheep and cattle; He scattered the coins of the money changers and overturned their tables. To those who sold doves He said, 'Get these out of here! Stop turning My Father's house into a market!' His disciples remembered that it is written: 'Zeal for Your house will consume me.'"

JOHN 2:13-17 NIV

THE FIRE OF GOD IN JESUS

To some, it was a place of worship. To others, it was a place of business to make a living by any means necessary. But to the Son, it was His Father's House—sacred ground and a place of prayer for the salvation, healing and deliverance of the nations. So, out came the whip against the money changers, the thieves and abusers, making the Pharisees fume with rage and risking His very life. But with the honor of His Father at stake and the deliverance of nations hanging in the balance, He laughed at death because it was all worth it. To the cross He would go, if He must. Oh, what a passion!

IN HUMAN EXPERIENCE, GOD'S FIRE TRANSLATES INTO passion—the type of passion we saw in Jesus. Perhaps He wasn't only passionate in His words. When Jesus was going to Jerusalem for the last time, we read that He was walking ahead of His disciples. They saw how He urged Himself onward. "Now they were on the road, going up to Jerusalem, and Jesus was going before them; and they were amazed. And as they followed they were afraid" (Mark 10:32). Why? Somehow, the fire in His soul was evident in the way He walked.

When they arrived, Jesus saw the desecration of the temple. The disciples then had further evidence of His passionate feelings. His reaction turned Him into an awesome figure. The disciples were reminded of the words of Psalm 69:9: "For zeal for Your house has consumed me..." But it was an anger born out of love, not a cold fury. Jesus was not a frenzied fanatic. He loved His Father's house, that's all. It was His desire to see people in the temple, worshipping with freedom and happiness. But commercialism in the temple had spoiled all that. His heart overflowed like a volcano. The fire of the Holy Spirit in His soul made Him cleanse the temple. His actions were frightening, and many fled from the scene because of them.

The children, the blind and the lame stayed though, and He healed them (Matthew 21:14-16). That was what He had wanted to do anyway, and that was the reason His anger achieved furnace-like heat. His indignation aimed for joy. He succeeded—the children ended up singing, "Hosanna!" This was the only occasion in Scripture where excitement about God was rebuked, the only time a hush was demanded in the courts of the Lord. The silence was demanded by the Pharisees—the praise of the Lord was drowning the tinkling of their commercial tills. Money music was muted! This was all part of the picture of the fire of the Lord—His consuming fire was designed to make way for exuberant praise.

DIVINE IMPERATIVE

"On the last day, that great day of the feast, Jesus stood and cried out, saying, 'If anyone thirsts, let him come to Me and drink. He who believes in Me, as the Scripture has said, out of his heart will flow rivers of living water."

JOHN 7:37, 38

FROM OLD TESTAMENT TO NEW TESTAMENT

> *What the Holy Spirit offers, no amount of good works or religion can provide. The Spirit of God satisfies every deep hunger and thirst. He brings refreshment and restoration to your soul in a way that nothing and nobody else can. If you are weary and need filling, Jesus bids you to come to Him, take a break and drink of the deep waters of the Holy Spirit (John 7:37, 38).*

THE MOST WONDERFUL SOUND EVER HEARD WAS ABOUT TO fall on the ears of thousands of people gathered in the temple courts at Jerusalem. The final rituals of a national festival were taking place. All eyes followed a golden vessel filled with water and wine. A drink offering was ready to be poured out to the Lord. A priest lifted the gleaming vessel in the sunshine and paused. Silence fell as the people strained to hear the sacred water splashing into a bronze bowl at the altar. Then came the interruption: a voice not known for 1,000 years a voice that made the spine tingle. It was the voice of Jesus Christ, the Son of God. He was the Word who had spoken in the beginning and called forth heaven and earth into existence. Now at Jerusalem, He stood and issued a royal and Divine edict, changing the dispensation of God: "If anyone thirsts, let him come to Me and drink. He who believes in Me, as the Scripture has said, out of his heart will flow rivers of living water" (John 7:37, 38). The age of the Holy Spirit had dawned.

SHOUT FOR JOY

> *The liberating effect of the Holy Spirit makes it very difficult and often impossible to keep your cool, and there is no need to. There is power in*

your shout. Give yourself the freedom to celebrate with ecstatic joy. Shout! There are rivers of joy flowing out of your innermost being! (John 7:38; 1 Peter 1:8).

RETURNING TO WHAT SCRIPTURE SAYS ABOUT THE HOLY Spirit, the word "rivers" is used repeatedly and describes the ideal for believers. Rivers are symbolic of the Holy Spirit. It was anticipated in Isaiah 58:11: "You shall be...like a spring of water, whose waters do not fail." A "rivers" experience requires the miracle presence of the Holy Spirit. For many people, exuberance is foreign, unnatural and embarrassing. For those, however, who stand within the Kingdom of God, the culture of the world matters little. In our Kingdom, people shout for joy. We only need to ask one question: If Christ did exactly what He promised and baptized people in the Holy Spirit and fire, what would they be like? Cool, restrained and self-contained? The emblem of God is fire, not a watermelon.

THE PRICE HAS BEEN PAID

"This only I want to learn from you: Did
you receive the Spirit by the works of the
law, or by the hearing of faith? Are you so
foolish? Having begun in the Spirit, are you
now being made perfect by the flesh?"

GALATIANS 3:2, 3

REPEL OR ATTRACT

Please note! Our weaknesses do not repel God; they attract Him. We may be hopeless, but the Spirit is God's gift specifically for the weak, to make up for our feebleness. "He gives power to the faint and to those who have no might, He increases strength" (Isaiah 40:29).

"AMAZING GRACE, HOW SWEET THE SOUND, THAT SAVED A wretch like me." At Calvary, there was a sound that brought salvation to humanity, and at Pentecost, there was another sound—the sound of a mighty rushing wind. It was the sound of zeal, of love, of the Spirit of God yearning for the embrace of humanity. Fully aware of the weaknesses of fallen humanity, the Holy Spirit came, and He is still here for you. Our sin sent Jesus to the cross, not our righteousness; our weakness brought the Holy Spirit down to us, not our perfection.

OUR WORTHINESS

Many Christians think that they are not worthy or good enough to receive the Holy Spirit. Yes, it is true that we will never be good enough for the Holy Spirit. But we do not have to be! Indeed, we cannot even hope to be. He is utterly holy. But that is why we need Him, and that is why He comes.

IT IS THE BLOOD OF JESUS. HIS BLOOD ALONE MAKES US worthy, and we are then answered by the power and infilling of the Holy Spirit (Acts 1:8). Christ sends the Spirit upon us—not because we are wonderful Christians, but precisely because we are not! God's heart is passionate for the salvation of His creatures. He did not make earth's billions as fuel for the flames of hell or to populate a cold

Christ-less eternity. He made them for heaven. He sends the Holy Spirit, the *Paraclete* or helper, and we are only His servants or His agents. He can do it—He only wants our cooperation.

WHAT ABOUT OUR HOLINESS?

> *Our holiness is not the power for signs and wonders. The Holy Spirit is the power. We may be weak and possibly stumbling, but that makes it even more necessary for us to receive the Holy Spirit. He is not given on condition that we are perfect. He is given because we are not perfect. THE BIGGEST FACTOR IS THAT WE NEED HIM. DO YOU NEED HIM?*

IF THE LOST CANNOT BE REACHED UNTIL THE CHURCH consists of perfect saints, when will they be reached? To win the lost cannot wait. Bringing them to Jesus will ensure that heaven is full and hell empty. God has made His greatest effort, His greatest sacrifice, for people to be saved, and He did not make it dependent on the extent of our perfection, waiting until we are a walking rule-book. We must seek holiness—and are encouraged by the Bible to do so—but the salvation of souls cannot wait until we reach perfection. God's plans always included the gift of the Spirit as the power-motive and the power-effects behind the Supreme Commission. There is no way without it.

THE OLD BATTERY

> *It does not matter how cold you are spiritually or how far you have wandered from the faith. Like an old battery, there is always a residual charge—once*

> *empowered by the Spirit, always empowered. You just must clean up with the Blood of Jesus, and you will be like brand new.*

A FRIEND OF MINE WAS CLEANING OUT HIS GARAGE AND tossed a piece of metal aside into what appeared to be a pile of garbage. It caused vivid and audible sparking. Investigation revealed an old car battery. The steel bar had shorted across its terminals. The cells still held some charge, so he brought it out for possible future use. For some, that might be a parable—you've given up, and think the power has gone. It never goes. Clear the rubbish out of the way and you will find that the Holy Spirit is not so easily switched off. After ministering under a strong prophetic unction for years, Elisha died, but the anointing remained on his bones. When a young man died and was accidentally thrown into Elisha's tomb, he came back to life (2 Kings 13:21). There is hope for you yet.

THE HOLY SPIRIT AND CALVARY

> *The Holy Spirit's purpose and focus is making the victories of the cross of Christ real in the believer, the Church and the world. To move in the power of the Holy Spirit, make the cross of Christ your business and salvation your message.*

THE HOLY SPIRIT IS ABSORBED IN HIS JOB. HE WORKS IN people's hearts what Jesus worked for us on the cross. You can't drag Him away from that place and get Him to attend to non–Calvary business. Only on redemption ground is there true spiritual power. Wonders without the cross are not Holy Spirit wonders.

FIRE POINTS

SECTION 3:

A MIGHTY RUSHING WIND–PENTECOST

A PROMISE FULFILLED

"When the Day of Pentecost had fully come,
they were all with one accord in one place. And
suddenly there came a sound from heaven, as of a
rushing, mighty wind, and it filled the whole house
where they were sitting. Then there appeared
to them divided tongues, as of fire, and one sat
upon each of them. And they were all filled with
the Holy Spirit and began to speak in other
tongues, as the Spirit gave them utterance."

ACTS 2:1-4

THE AGE OF THE HOLY SPIRIT HAS COME

The coming of the Holy Spirit changed the world order and tipped the scales in favor of the Church. But there is one major difference—only the Kingdom of God can have access to this almighty power. No rogue nation, no axis of evil...Just us!

THE AGE OF THE HOLY SPIRIT HAS COME. WHEN JESUS SENT the Holy Spirit into the world, it was a cosmic event which could not be undone. It created a new order of possibilities beyond all that had been known since the days of Adam. A new form of life—resurrection life—was now available. Resurrection life is like radiation—not contaminating nuclear radiation, but resurrection radiation. The same Spirit that raised Jesus from the dead will raise us also into a life of spiritual elevation and power (Romans 8:11).

THE ARRIVAL OF THE HOLY SPIRIT

To bring salvation, the Holy Spirit took residence in Christ the Lord, but to preach salvation, the Holy Spirit takes residence in the Church—men and women, young and old, from all nations and tribes, cleansed with the precious blood of the Lamb.

THE HOLY SPIRIT ANNOUNCED HIS ARRIVAL IN JERUSALEM through 120 throats and wrapped Himself in the flesh of the disciples. We are His temples, His residential address here on earth. From that moment, the lives of the disciples were never the same. As they radiated the glory of God with courage, healings, miracles, prophetic signs and wonders, people took notice that they had been with Jesus (Acts 2), because the same Holy Spirit by which Jesus operated was upon them. The Holy Spirit took residence in the church and has not withdrawn. That same Holy Spirit is with us, in us and working through us today.

IT'S FOR ALL

The Holy Spirit is not distributed by lottery, with a few people selected to receive. It is not a game of chance. There are no winners or losers. Those whom God calls, He equips. There is more than enough power to go around. No one is left out, and no one gets leftovers. Don't disqualify yourself when you are already accepted.

THE SCRIPTURES ARE CLEAR AND WITHOUT VAGUENESS. The baptism in the Holy Spirit is not just for a few of "God's favorites." No, God has no "favorites." In fact, we are all His favorites. On the Day of Pentecost, 120 men and women were in the Upper Room in Jerusalem, and we read in Acts 2:3 and 4, "Then there appeared to them divided tongues, as of fire, and one sat upon each of them. And they were all filled with the Holy Spirit..." It was no coincidence and NO LOTTERY! "Each" of the 120 received and "all" were filled. Their gender was not a consideration, neither was their age nor race nor status in life. You qualify for the Holy Spirit baptism! IT IS FOR ALL God's blood-washed children, including you and me. God's power is unlimited; He does not run out of gas, and He has more than enough power for all of His people—all who hunger and thirst.

A FLAME FOR YOUR HEAD

There were 120 people in the Upper Room. Somebody in heaven must have counted the heads, since one flame landed "on each of them." If you have a head, God has a flame for you. Right now, His count includes you. "You shall receive power..." (Acts 1:8). Just imagine, your head becomes a landing strip for the fire of the Holy Spirit. He lands and abides—never to take off again.

EVERY ONE OF THE 120 DISCIPLES IN THE UPPER ROOM ON the Day of Pentecost received the baptism of the Holy Spirit. No one was left out. It was not just for the 12 apostles that we know or that walked closely with Jesus. There were nameless ones that also received. They may not have been famous, but they were faithful. They showed up in the Upper Room and waited for the promise. The Holy Spirit came upon all, and a flame of fire landed on top of all their heads—120 flames for 120 faithful ones. If you show up, you will have a flame of power for your assignment.

PACEMAKER

The Holy Spirit brings us into divine alignment and enables us to walk in step and in sync with God's plans and purposes, following His Kingdom agenda. Romans 8:14 says, "For as many as are led by the Spirit of God, these are the sons of God."

A PACEMAKER IS A SMALL DEVICE THAT'S PLACED IN THE chest or abdomen to help control abnormal heart rhythms. I believe that the flame of the Holy Spirit on every believer is something like a pacemaker. It corrects abnormal rhythms and brings us into harmony with the heart of God. His agenda or ours? His will or ours? The flame on my head, carrying my name, makes me march to the rhythm of God's heartbeat.

THE HOLY SPIRIT'S INCARNATION

As the Father sent the Son to save us, so He sends His Spirit to fill and empower us. The Holy Spirit does not come because we deserve it; He comes because of the Father's love, the Son's sacrifice and our need for a Helper and Comforter. We don't need to perform, just receive.

ON THE DAY OF PENTECOST, THEY BEGAN TO PREACH THE Gospel "by the Holy Spirit sent from heaven" (1 Peter 1:12). His was a positive descent and entrance into the world, as much as when Jesus came from heaven. "The Word became flesh" (John 1:14)—that was Jesus' entrance through the door of Bethlehem. He clothed Himself with human form and, similarly, the Holy Spirit garbed Himself with the disciples as He took up residence within them. The world could not receive Him, but hundreds loved Jesus, and a group of 120 of them became the first Spirit-filled people on earth—men, women, apostles and disciples. They were simply sitting together, not standing, kneeling or praying, just waiting as Jesus had instructed them: "Do not leave Jerusalem, but wait for the gift My Father promised" (Acts 1:4 NIV). Christ ascended to heaven and asked the Father to send His gift, the Holy Spirit. Within 10 days, He had come.

TOGETHER AS ONE

At Pentecost, God and man rejoiced together as one in the charismatic language. To "speak with tongues" (Acts 2) means the Bride has been taken into the embrace of the Divine Bridegroom (Colossians 2:9-10).

THE GREAT DIVIDE BETWEEN GOD AND HUMANITY REACHED its peak at Babel when God came down and confused the language of mankind (Genesis 11:1-9). What God did at Babel, He reversed at Pentecost, uniting them by different languages. From all walks of life, races and cultures, He has purchased us with His blood (Revelation 5:9, 10) and has united us—not to build a tower to man's glory or ingenuity but to build a Kingdom to the glory of God. By the Holy Spirit, humanity and God rejoice, celebrating this grand reunion together in one blessed language.

PROPHETIC EVANGELISM

"And there were dwelling in Jerusalem Jews, devout men, from every nation under heaven. And when this sound occurred, the multitude came together, and were confused, because everyone heard them speak in his own language. Then they were all amazed and marveled, saying to one another, 'Look, are not all these who speak Galileans? And how is it that we hear, each in our own language in which we were born?...We hear them speaking in our own tongues the wonderful works of God.' So they were all amazed and perplexed, saying to one another, 'Whatever could this mean?'"

ACTS 2:5-12

FIRE AND FLESH

The Spirit wants to make a connection. On the Day of Pentecost, the tongue of fire on the heads of those in the Upper Room connected with the tongue of flesh in their mouths, and the result was a glorious and powerful prophetic, cross-cultural evangelistic outburst that transformed the believers and changed the world.

APOSTLE JAMES GIVES US SOME VERY POWERFUL INSIGHT about the human tongue, saying that we often curse others and bless God with the same mouth (James 3). But on the Day of Pentecost, as ordinary men and women yielded to God, their tongues became instruments of power and salvation. The tongue of fire on their heads connected with the tongue of flesh in their mouths. The heavenly connected with the earthly, the supernatural with the natural. "...And they began to speak in other tongues as the Spirit gave them utterance" (Acts 2:4).

SAVING TRUTH

Since the Day of Pentecost, God speaks through human voices—as the Holy Spirit gives them UTTERANCE. This was more than inspiration. The first believers were all filled with the Holy Spirit. Speakers FOR God are speaking BY God—with THRUST. It is a door "of UTTERANCE" (Colossians 4:3 KJV). True preaching is SAVING-PREACHING. The Holy Spirit endows preaching with His power to save souls from the devil. "His Word was in my heart like a burning fire..." (Jeremiah 20:9).

WE READ THAT ON THE DAY OF PENTECOST, "THEN THERE appeared to them divided tongues as of fire and one sat upon each of them...and they began to speak in other tongues, as the Spirit gave them UTTERANCE" (Acts 2:3, 4). The Holy Spirit transformed the prayers, praises and preaching of the disciples with vibrancy. The praises of the disciples, filled with wonder, passion and power, cut across ethnic and racial boundaries (Acts 2:5-12). Religious people, whose form of worship was cold and liturgical, experienced for the first time a new wave of Holy Spirit-invigorated worship and praise. Peter preached with unprecedented boldness and conviction, and 3,000 people were saved and added to the Church that day.

GOD'S ETHNIC INTEREST

God's heart has been and always will be for the nations—for all peoples. He does not desire that any should perish but that all will come to the knowledge of the truth (2 Peter 3:9). The Holy Spirit wants to empower you to impact the nations: peoples from every tribe, race and culture. Work for God wherever you are, but pray for a global harvest. Don't be afraid to cross cultural and geographical boundaries.

WHEN THE HOLY SPIRIT FELL AT PENTECOST, THE JEWISH disciples did not speak in Hebrew but in the languages of people from many distant countries (Acts 2:8-12), displaying the ethnic interest of God's Spirit and erasing any doubt of His love and hope for all peoples. Pentecost fulfilled God's promise through Joel, that in the last days He would pour out His Spirit on everyone (Joel 2:28-32). God desires to release His Spirit on all people. This is consistent with the Gospel, "For God so loved the world that He gave His only begotten Son, that whosoever believes in Him should not perish but have everlasting life" (John 3:16). It makes sense that a God who gave His Son for all would give His Spirit to all. He gave His Son for our salvation and His Spirit for our empowerment.

THE GOSPEL OF PENTECOST

"But Peter, standing up with the eleven, raised his voice and said to them...'Men of Israel, hear these words: Jesus of Nazareth, a Man attested by God to you by miracles, wonders and signs which God did through Him in your midst, as you yourselves also know—Him, being delivered by the determined purpose and foreknowledge of God, you have taken by lawless hands, have crucified, and put to death; whom God raised up, having loosed the pains of death, because it was not possible that He should be held by it...Repent, and let every one of you be baptized in the name of Jesus Christ for the remission of sins; and you shall receive the gift of the Holy Spirit.'"

ACTS 2:14, 22-24, 38

HOLY SPIRIT BOLDNESS

> *When the Holy Spirit comes upon you, you don't just receive power to perform signs. He strengthens you physically, psychologically and emotionally. The baptism of the Spirit imputes boldness; the weakest coward can be transformed into the most courageous and heroic person.*

IT WAS NOT JUST SEEING JESUS OR HEARING HIS VOICE THAT made the disciples the bold people they later were—even some of them doubted (Matthew 28:17; Mark 16:13-14; Luke 24:41). They shut the door when they met for fear of the Jews (John 20:19). They met secretly, being too afraid to have a street procession shouting, "Jesus is alive!" At first, far away in Galilee, they even went back to their old jobs—fishing (John 21:3). All that changed, however, on the Day of Pentecost when they received the Holy Spirit baptism and boldness. Instead of being afraid of the Jewish crowds, the crowds trembled before them and cried out, "Men and brethren, what shall we do?" (Acts 2:37). This was the fulfillment of what Jesus said: "But you shall receive power when the Holy Spirit has come upon you; and you shall be witnesses to Me...to the end of the earth" (Acts 1:8).

HOLY SPIRIT PURPOSE

> *For what purpose did the Father send the Holy Spirit? Without any question, it is to make it possible to preach the Gospel to every creature on earth.*

PAUL DESCRIBES IT AS BRINGING THE NATIONS INTO THE obedience of the Gospel (Romans 1:5). The consuming passion and work of Christ was "to seek and to save that which was lost" (Luke

19:10). Jesus was never just a wonder-worker. First and foremost, He was and is the Savior. It was that work which took Him to the Cross. That was the ultimate purpose of His earthly life. It was not for some social good—just to feed multitudes—but for the redemption of humankind. This was foremost in His mind. Any talk of 'greater works' has to be in line with His own 'great work' to save the lost. Salvation is the greatest labor and the greatest marvel God ever undertook.

THE HOLY SPIRIT AS BIBLE INTERPRETER

The Holy Spirit illuminates the Scriptures, bringing understanding to the Word of God and revealing mysteries hidden in Scripture. Without the Author of the Bible to shed light on the Word, we are reduced to guesswork.

THE GOLDEN RULE IN BIBLE INTERPRETATION IS THAT WHICH Paul himself shared in 1 Corinthians 2:12-13: "...That we might know the things that have been freely given to us by God. These things we also speak, not in words which man's wisdom teaches, but which the Holy Spirit teaches; comparing spiritual things with spiritual." The word translated "spiritual things" here is the same word translated "spiritual gifts" in 1 Corinthians 12:1—*pneumatika*. Understanding the Bible is not a matter of guesswork. Simply make use of the Bible interpreter, the Holy Spirit.

NO COMMITTEE

One man filled with the Holy Spirit is better than 100 committees, which, as someone said, "keep minutes but lose hours." When God so loved the world, He did not form a committee; He sent His Son, and His Son sent the Holy Spirit (John 3:16; Luke 24:49). Christ said that believers are the light of the world, but we need the Holy Spirit to switch us on. Are you plugged in?

ON THE DAY OF PENTECOST, PETER STOOD UP, SHOOK OFF his shame and fears, and shared the only theology he knew—Jesus and Him crucified. Thus, 3,000 were saved from diverse nations without a committee, budget or finance meeting. That is the power of the Holy Spirit; He makes the Gospel come alive and brings conviction en masse. If we pay more attention to the Holy Spirit, we will spend less time in planning committees and see more results.

A FIRE COMBINATION

"Jesus answered them...'No one can come
to Me unless the Father Who sent Me draws
him...it is the Spirit who gives life; the flesh
profits nothing. The words that I speak
to you are spirit, and they are life.'"

JOHN 6:44, 63

THE GOSPEL & THE HOLY SPIRIT—
A FIRE COMBINATION

> *By all means, preach the truth of the Gospel. There is no nobler task and no better commission than this, but without the power of the Holy Spirit, it is reduced to mere words, facts, history and commentary. It is as useless to saving souls as a newspaper on a derailed passenger train.*

TRUTH IS WONDERFUL, BUT OF ITSELF, IT IS DEAD. IT IS LIKE coal in the shed. We need more than orthodox Bible-teaching. Coal only releases its energy in combination with fire, and the fire of the Holy Spirit is needed to set truth ablaze! (Luke 24:32). Jesus said, "The words that I speak to you are spirit, and they are life" (John 6:63). Baptized by the Holy Spirit, the message Jesus preached was more than mere words; it carried life and conviction, and 2,000 years later it is still changing the lives of billions of people all over the world.

THE SECRET OF THE GOSPEL

> *The Holy Spirit powers the Gospel as electricity powers a water station. However, we do not generate Holy Spirit power by prayer, sweat, agony, time, effort, good works or anything else. The Father gives us the Spirit as a gift, not a reward or wages—something we earn.*

IT IS HIGH TIME FOR US TO UNDERSTAND WHO THE HOLY Spirit is: the secret of Gospel-power. It is not a case of struggling and sweating to get the Spirit but of just letting Him come in. We do not manufacture His power or make Him effective; it is the gift of God

(Luke 11:13). No good works are required. If we could make ourselves so good that we deserved the Holy Spirit, we would not need Him.

HAND IN GLOVE

> *Without the power of the Holy Spirit, the Gospel is empty and ineffectual. It has a form of godliness, but it is void of its power to save and transform.*

THE GOSPEL IS NOT A HUMAN INVENTION OR ASSIGNMENT. God is the Author of the Gospel, and then He commissioned humanity to tell the world. The Holy Spirit is like the hand in the glove of the preached Gospel. The Gospel must be preached under Divine unction; then, any result can be achieved. It is the power that can ensure the Great Commission is fulfilled.

TRANSFER OF FIRE

> *The Gospel is nothing less than the voice of God. When that Gospel is preached by a Holy Spirit-filled person or in a Flame Church, people will hear. The Gospel becomes a transfer of fire from God. Without the Gospel and without fire, however clever or magnificent the setting, it leaves hearers cold and dead. Pomp is not power. The Spirit makes the Word alive (John 6:63).*

THIS IS NO OLYMPIC TORCH. THIS IS THE BURNING TORCH OF the fire of the Holy Spirit passed from eternity to time and from generation to generation. The fire Moses saw now rested on the disciples; from the burning bush (Exodus 3:1, 2), it ignited the altar of

Solomon (2 Chronicles 7:1) and landed at Pentecost on the disciples' heads (Acts 2:3). The fire of God Himself, in tongues of flames now leaping on each head, not appearing as a mere spectacle or manifestation but an experience—God and man together. He is the God of fire and burning. We live in a spiritually dark and cold world. The best way to keep from freezing is to be aglow with the Holy Spirit. God will light a fire on the altar of your own heart so that you can be a firelighter.

A LIGHT TO THE GENTILES

"Indeed He says, 'It is too small a thing that You should be My Servant to raise up the tribes of Jacob, and to restore the preserved ones of Israel; I will also give You as a light to the Gentiles, that You should be My salvation to the ends of the earth.'"

ISAIAH 49:6

HEALING OF THE NATIONS

The healing of the nations is found in the preaching of the Word by the Spirit of the living God. But it starts with us. We must go, but as we go, we must believe the Word, be touched with the power of the Spirit and be set free ourselves. Burning hot, we will become God's healing agents, like the Good Samaritan in the dusty roads of the world, healing the victims of the devil.

"SO THEN FAITH COMES BY HEARING, AND HEARING BY THE Word of God" (Romans 10:17). When the Holy Spirit illuminates scriptures to you, it sparks faith and challenges you to act upon the Word. My own faith began as the Holy Spirit used Bible texts like burning arrows, setting my mind on fire. For example, Revelation 22:2 states that the tree of life has leaves for "the healing of the nations." The Word of God became my tree of life, and the leaves of that book appeared to me like heavenly medicine. Praise God!

CONQUERING THE CONQUERORS

Jesus said, "I have come to bring fire to earth" (Luke 12:49 NIV). His followers caught a burning faith. "The disciples went out and preached everywhere, and the Lord worked with them..." (Mark 16:20 NIV). They set the dark, cold pagan world aflame and melted the iron eagle emblem of the Roman Empire, conquering the conquerors.

EMPERORS BOWED THEIR KNEES TO JESUS, THE ONE THEY had crucified as a criminal. Nothing but power from God could affect such marvels. The secret was humble people flaming for God, fire-baptized. They had fire then, but is that fire only seen in candles today? Is that apostolic succession? If we are in the lineage of the apostles, there should be some similarity to validate the claim besides ornate robes. We need the true apostolic mantle. Today, many people go to church only to "hatch, match and dispatch" (birth, marriage and funeral). But dead and dry things are easier to catch fire. Peter said, "For the promise is to you and your children and for all who are afar off" (Acts 2:39). We qualify. We are far off.

GOD OF THE NATIONS

Your calling is beyond yourself and your immediate surroundings. It is to the world. The harvest fields are the nations. Don't let your environment smother your vision and your fire. Open your eyes and look beyond your circles and your personal struggles. The world is ripe for harvest (Luke 10:2).

AFTER CHRIST ROSE FROM THE DEAD, THE DISCIPLES RETAINED a Jewish outlook for a long time. They saw their new faith as belonging only to Israel. They even asked the Lord, an hour or so before He ascended, "'Lord, will You at this time restore the kingdom of Israel?' And He said to them, 'It is not for you to know times or seasons, which the Father has put in His own authority. But you shall receive power when the Holy Spirit has come upon you; and you shall be witnesses to Me in Jerusalem, and in all Judea and Samaria, and to the end of the earth'" (Acts 1:6-8). Jesus wanted His disciples to reach the world and not just Judea. They were starting out from Jerusalem, but their destination was the nations.

FIRE POINTS

SECTION 4:

DIPPED IN FIRE–THE BAPTISM OF THE HOLY SPIRIT

THE LATTER RAIN

"At that day you will know that I am in My
Father, and you in Me, and I in you."

JOHN 14:20

TOTALLY UNMATCHED

> *The baptism in the Holy Spirit is not insignificant, common or incidental. It is not a mere religious gesture—a hand waved to bless us. It is unmatched. It is the exclusive promise of Jesus Christ, and He alone has ever given it. It is wonderful, and it is the hard evidence of what He has done for us. JESUS is the "Baptizer in the Spirit" (Matthew 3:11). That is one of His most blessed works.*

THE BAPTISM OF THE HOLY SPIRIT IS NOT SYMBOLIC OR ceremonious—simply religious jargon to be used in church liturgy or congregational worship. It is the power of the Holy Spirit sent to empower the Church for its earthly assignment. Without it, no souls can be saved no matter our efforts. No lasting change can occur in, with or through the Church apart from the Holy Spirit. Without the baptism of the Holy Spirit, the Church is outmatched by the darkness that pervades the earth and by the tricks of the enemy (John 16: 13).

BLOWING THROUGH OUR STUFFY TRADITIONS

> *We may sing "Welcome, welcome, Holy Spirit," but He does not come because of our welcome. He is no guest or stranger invited in for an hour or two. He is the Lord of heaven, and He invites us into His presence. Where there is faith and the Word, He finds His natural environment.*

THE APOSTLES WERE NOT PRAYING FOR THE SPIRIT, BUT HE came and invaded the place. Any atmosphere they might have experienced together was blown away, invaded by a "rushing mighty wind" (Acts 2:2). The Spirit is the atmosphere of heaven itself, and heaven comes down here with Him. He is the *pneuma*, the wind of heaven, blowing through our stuffy traditions and stagnation and bringing times of refreshing on all.

BRIDGE FROM HEAVEN TO EARTH

> *Being baptized in the Holy Spirit is like being in one long continuum of the latter rain (Joel 2:23, 28, 29), connecting the heavens and the earth with life-giving rivers of blessing—producing fruit and ending drought.*

THE BAPTISM IN THE SPIRIT IS A BRIDGE BETWEEN EARTH AND heaven for everyone. Micah 5:7 says that the Lord will come down like "showers on the grass." Perhaps on a stormy day, when you have been in the countryside, you have noticed a rainstorm in the distance. The sky is purple, full of storm clouds. Beneath it is a wall of rain reaching from the sky to the ground. It links the cloudy sky with the ground, the heavens with the earth. Those clouds (the heavens), the rain falling and the floods on the earth are one and the same. Heaven and earth are united. When we are filled with the Spirit, it is "the latter rain."

SUPERNATURAL LINK

> *When we are baptized in the Spirit, we are brought into the same reality as we will know in heaven. The Holy Spirit is the Holy One; He manifests God supernaturally and Divinely as well as physically. Holy Spirit baptism links us to heaven in a way we have never experienced before.*

THE HOLY SPIRIT HAS ALWAYS BEEN THE ONE WHO BROUGHT the operation of God down to us. He is that link between heaven and earth. When we are baptized in the Holy Spirit, the Gospel is brought home to the children of earth. We get into God's storm clouds of the latter rain. We are soaked in the Spirit. Wherever we go after we have been in the Upper Room, we will carry signs and evidences of it. God will be with us in a new way, making it hard to conceal the signs. Our lights will shine as we meet all travelers on the road. And we will not be alone, for others coming behind us will carry the same signs of a supernatural link to heaven.

HEAVEN REMAINS OPEN

The door to heaven is open and will remain open. Your prayers cannot be blocked and neither can the answers. You have full access to the throne of grace; "Therefore come boldly...that we may obtain mercy and find grace in time of need" (Hebrews 4:16). There are no more hindrances.

BOTH DAVID AND ISAIAH PRAYED, "LORD, REND THE HEAVENS and come down" (Psalm 144:5; Isaiah 64:1). It happened when Jesus came. New Testament believers need never pray that again. Christ tore open the heavens and came down to us. He then returned through the heavens, ensuring that they will remain open. The rent heavens have been rent forever; they have never been sewn up again, neither by a needle-wielding Satan nor by any other hand. Through that open heaven, the Holy Spirit began to descend—the latter rain. The heavens are no more like brass. Hell cannot impose sanctions and blockade the Kingdom of God. It has no power to deprive God's citizens. The new and living way is established beyond enemy control.

HOLY SPIRIT DYNAMISM

"The wind blows where it wishes, and you
hear the sound of it, but cannot tell where
it comes from and where it goes. So is
everyone who is born of the Spirit."

JOHN 3:8

AIR IN A JAR IS NOT WIND

> *The mighty, rushing wind blew into the Upper Room on the Day of Pentecost and didn't stop. Since Pentecost, the Holy Spirit is constantly moving and working, bringing refreshing and empowerment to the Church. The Spirit of God took the field long ago, and He has never withdrawn from the battle! He does not "visit" now and then: He came to stay permanently.*

ON-GOING PENTECOST! WHAT IS IT? IT IS WHAT BEGAN WHEN JESUS ASCENDED through the gates of glory: He left the door open. Then the HOLY SPIRIT DESCENDED through the same opening (Acts 7:56). A strong breeze began blowing—a mighty, rushing wind. It blew away the stale air of musty religious tradition. They needed no air-conditioner in the Upper Room; it was filled with the freshness of Resurrection springtime.

The Holy Spirit is always on the move, always in action. The New Testament word for Spirit is *pneuma*, meaning wind or breath—air in motion. *Pneuma* does NOT mean still air. Have you ever known a wind that didn't blow? To be wind, it must be in motion. I never heard of a "still hurricane" or a "calm gale." Air in a jar is not wind. If the Holy Spirit is wind, then He is in motion all the time or He is not the Holy Spirit. To ask the Holy Spirit to move is like asking for fire to be hot. The idea of a Holy Spirit who doesn't move is unknown in Scripture. The Holy Spirit always means Divine activity. He is the Divine Operator on earth.

PREVAILING WINDS FROM HEAVEN

> *Weathermen speak of the prevailing wind. The winds change, but there is always a normal or general direction, such as from the west. The air currents*

naturally flow in that direction. There is also a prevailing wind from heaven. The Holy Spirit constantly blows with the pure freshness of glory, day and night, always streaming toward us.

WE ALL TALK ABOUT GOD MOVING ON OUR BEHALF IN answer to prayer. He does, but there is something else. He is always moving. God moves TOWARD us, all the time, with prevailing currents of blessing and power. God does not come in gusts, such as an occasional sudden blast on a Sunday morning or Friday night prayer meeting. His sovereign will is nothing like that. His will is what Scripture teaches—that God isn't a weak force one day and a strong force the next day. We need no barometer for God and no temperature gauge. He isn't around sometimes for revival or healing, but all the time—it is up to us, not God, Who never changes. He doesn't have moods. God has no uncertainty factor; it is our faith that has to push past uncertainty.

NO SPURTS OF POWER

The New Testament makes no distinctions in the work of God. Scripture never talks in terms of special "moves" of God, spurts of power or revival spasms. Christianity is a Holy Spirit movement from start to finish. The Spirit of God is always moving and always reviving His work.

IN SCRIPTURE, WE READ ABOUT THE POOL OF BETHESDA, where an angel would stir the waters every now and then (John 5:1-9). Whoever could get into the pool first would be healed. The pool offered a solution, but it was not a constant flow, and it was very competitive to access. A man lay by the pool for 38 years and was never healed—until he met Jesus. Whenever the waters were stirred, he could never get in quickly enough. Jesus' love, mercies and power are not like the pool of Bethesda. They are constant and never switched off. They are independent of our personal efforts; all He asks is whether we want to receive.

ON THE GO FOR GOD

> *The on-going Holy Spirit needs on-going people. Pentecost is a driving energy by its very definition. The Spirit is ceaselessly moving. Matthew 28:10 is clear about the purpose for the wind of the Holy Spirit. "GO, TELL MY BRETHREN!"*

ON-GOING PENTECOST MUST BE PENTECOST WITH A GO, and we must do the GOING and the TELLING. As soon as we gather, He is there to bless, to heal and to save. Evangelism by the Holy Spirit is a gale of freshness blowing through the dirty atmosphere of our streets. We only need to partner with the Holy Spirit and let His wind blow!

THE OVERFLOW

"...You anoint my head with oil;
My cup overflows."

PSALM 23:5 NIV

NO DEPOT – BUT DIRECT

> *In Christ we have access to renewable energy. There's no such thing as a power failure. You can never use up God's power. The Holy Spirit continues to energize us as the vine energizes the branches—moment by moment.*

ACTS 2 SAYS THAT ON THE DAY OF PENTECOST, THE DISCIPLES were filled with the Holy Spirit, and the rest of the book shows how they continued. They went on being filled, "moment by moment," as the song-writer says. "Moment by moment I'm kept in His love, moment by moment I've life from above. Looking to Jesus..." This means that He is the vine, and we are the branches. We get our supplies afresh daily from Him. Jesus described it as continuous as a river (John 7:37, 38). We are being renewed in spiritual power as we need and use it.

UNINTERRUPTED FLOW

> *"God does not give the Spirit by measure"(John 3:34) when He gives it. Not by measure means not weighed—not precisely so much and no more—but "good measure, pressed down, shaken together and running over" (Luke 6:38). God never gives anything in a calculating manner. For example, He gives life, but it is without measure—BECAUSE IT IS HIS LIFE and it is EVERLASTING (John 3:36).*

ELISHA'S DOUBLE PORTION WAS NOT JUST A BIT OF WHAT Elijah had. God never arranges for some to have half and some twice as much as others. The Holy Spirit gives "of" (out of) Himself, out of His fullness, not a measured gallon or two. The Bible promised showers and rivers, not drops. Powerful rivers don't come by fits and starts, and rivers, not drops. Powerful rivers don't come by fits and starts, dribs and drabs, nor does the Holy Spirit come as an occasional spurt. Christ chose the expression of "rivers" to indicate uninterrupted flow (John 7:37, 38).

HARD EVIDENCE

"And these signs will follow those who believe:
In My name they will cast out demons; they
will speak with new tongues; they will take up
serpents; and if they drink anything deadly,
it will by no means hurt them; they will lay
hands on the sick, and they will recover."

MARK 16:17, 18

A PILLAR OF FIRE

> At Pentecost, the Holy Spirit manifested like a tongue of flame on each of
> the 120 disciples present. It was a sign of Divine presence and empowerment.
> Divine fire was given for Divine commission and protection.

FIRE IS THE SIGN OF GOD—HIS LOGO. THERE ARE OVER 100 references in Scripture to the fire of God. "Our God is a consuming fire" (Hebrews 12:29). Two of the greatest spiritual events were inaugurated by Divine fire: the beginning of the nation of Israel at the Exodus and the beginning of the Church with tongues of fire. A curtain of fire hung between Israel and the Egyptians at the Exodus, like a banner assuring Israel that the Lord of hosts was with them. The assurance that God is with us is the same today. The tongues of Pentecost signal that God is with us. Jesus said, "I came to send fire on the earth" (Luke 12:49). Like a fire-tipped arrow, God shoots you into the camp of the enemy to bring salvation to the captives.

THE SIGN–GIFT IS A BENCHMARK

> The Holy Spirit Baptism is a permanent and total revolution in the life of the
> Church. The Spirit falling on all people was the greatest change possible. The
> benchmark is a sign-gift. It was a revelation. They knew power had come; the
> Holy Spirit was with them, and they never asked for Him again. The same
> Holy Spirit sign was accepted by the apostles: "And they were all filled with
> the Holy Spirit and began to speak with other tongues, as the Spirit gave them
> utterance" (Acts 2:4). There is no other power except the Holy Spirit. This
> sign-miracle proved that any miracle is possible.

THROUGHOUT TIME, MEN AND WOMEN HAVE ALWAYS demanded or been given signs to boost their faith. After the floods of Noah, God gave the rainbow as a sign that there would never again be a worldwide deluge (Genesis 9:12-17). While still childless, God gave Abraham a sign to assure him that he would be a father of many nations (Genesis 15). Praying in tongues is a sign but not an empty one. It is dynamic, supernatural proof that speaks to the presence of the Holy Spirit in the believer. It reassures our faith, but it is also a means for communicating; it helps us as we pray, sing, prophesy and minister. Tongues is also a benchmark, marking a new season in God's dealing with humanity: "In the last days, I will pour out my Spirit on all flesh" (Acts 2:17).

ENDORSEMENT

> *Speaking in tongues is a sign of the presence and power of the Holy Spirit in your life. It introduces certainty into the dynamics of the Spirit, making a spiritual phenomenon a natural and personal experience. Pentecost means: God and man rejoice together as one in the charismatic language.*

"UTTERANCE" IS AN ENDORSING SIGN THAT THE HOLY SPIRIT IS in and with us. Otherwise, we can never be certain. (Have I prayed enough? Am I holy enough? Have I witnessed enough?) But God shaped us for His Spirit. The baptism in the Spirit is a physical and spiritual event (1 Corinthians 6:19) with both a spiritual and physical sign.

THE POSSIBILITY SIGN!

> *Next to salvation of the soul, praying in tongues is the most wondrous phenomenon of all. What can be more powerful than the regenerated spirit of*

mortal man quickened and made righteous, speaking in a heavenly language with his Father? Praying in tongues proves that there is nothing impossible.

ON THE DAY OF PENTECOST, THE 120 SPOKE IN TONGUES, AND the crowd listened and was shaken. In my life, I have witnessed how 1 million people, in one meeting, received the same fire baptism and prayed to the Lord in new languages by the Spirit. It was like the roar of mighty waters. "And it shall come to pass in the last days,' says God, 'that I will pour out of My Spirit on all flesh...'" (Acts 2:17). These are the days!

FIRE POINTS

SECTION 5:

TOOLS OF FIRE–THE GIFTS AND POWER OF THE HOLY SPIRIT

PRECIOUS AND PRICELESS

"And when Jesus was in Bethany at the house of Simon the leper, a woman came to Him having an alabaster flask of very costly fragrant oil, and she poured it on His head as He sat at the table. But when His disciples saw it, they were indignant, saying, 'Why this waste? For this fragrant oil might have been sold for much and given to the poor.' But when Jesus was aware of it, He said to them, 'Why do you trouble the woman? For she has done a good work for Me.'"

MATTHEW 26:6-10

ONLY AN EMPTY SHELL?

> THE HOLY SPIRIT is not an accessory, but the very substance of what we believe. He is God on earth, actively indwelling and saturating every particle of what we experience. This means that Christianity is a supernatural faith. A non-supernatural Gospel is an empty shell.

MANY BELIEVERS TREAT THE HOLY SPIRIT AS THOUGH HE IS optional—a suggestion they can dismiss and still be okay as Christians. No! He is not an addendum to the Christian experience; He is the author of it, sustaining it through the millennia before and after Christ. He is the Host; without Him, there is no banquet. We ignore Him at our own peril. The Holy Spirit was there in the beginning and shall be after the ending. He is Alpha and Omega, and we need to pay attention if we want to run our race and finish our course.

LOVE'S WASTEFUL EXTRAVAGANCE

> The anointing of the Spirit is not a second-rate experience, sent to appease or pacify your conscience that you have some Divine goodness in you. No, it is the real deal: God's best. It is He Himself. We have received it through the crucified Christ, who broke the most expensive alabaster box of all, His Body, pouring the precious fragrance on humanity.

THE FRAGRANCE OF MARY'S OIL WAS SO RICH THAT IT pervaded the whole house. It was a tremendous sacrifice and an act of love's wasteful extravagance. It speaks of the love of God, through Jesus Christ, which brings us the priceless gift of the anointing of the Holy Spirit. It is no cheap experience but God's best. When Christ went to the cross of Calvary, His body, the most precious sacrifice of all, was given. With it, He released the priceless fragrance of the Holy Spirit and all of God's Divine goodness on humanity.

SHEDDING HIS FRAGRANCE ABROAD

God breathed into the Word, like a flower drinking in the wind and sunshine. Then the flower breathes the sunshine out again, transformed into beauty and fragrance. We call this process photosynthesis. Something like spiritual photosynthesis should take place in every Christian life. "Be filled with the Spirit" (Ephesians 5:18), and it won't show in just religious devotion, but also in loveliness of character as you shed His fragrance abroad.

THE CHIEF WORK OF THE HOLY SPIRIT IS US! HE MAKES US HIS agents. A little girl once prayed "Dear Lord, please make all bad people good and all good people nice." She somehow must have observed, that "good" is not necessarily "nice." God grant that we are both! That is the way the world will know about Him.

GIFTS, NOT PURCHASES

"And when Simon saw that through the laying on of the apostles' hands the Holy Spirit was given, he offered them money, saying, 'Give me this power also, that anyone on whom I lay hands may receive the Holy Spirit.' But Peter said to him, 'May your money perish with you, because you thought that the gift of God could be purchased with money!'"

ACTS 8:18-20

UNDERSTANDING THE PERSON OF THE HOLY SPIRIT

> *It is necessary to understand that the Holy Spirit is He, not "it." The Spirit is not an impersonal force—a sort of spiritual electricity. The anointing of God is not just power or gifts, but the Holy Spirit Himself.*

VARIOUS ELEMENTS ARE USED TO DESCRIBE THE HOLY SPIRIT in Scripture: fire, wind, water. But it is important to realize that the Holy Spirit is not an inanimate element but rather a person. He is not a force, like the gravitational pull of the universe or a current of electricity. He is the Third Person of the Holy Trinity. Neither His gifts nor the fruit of the Spirit are to be separated from Him. You have all of God, not just His gifts.

A PRICE TO PAY FOR THE GIFTS?

> *Is there a price to pay for the gifts? If there is, they would not be gifts but purchases (Acts 8:18-20). Nevertheless, there well may be a price to pay in their use. Those not prepared to risk their leisure, their comfort, their reputation and perhaps much more may be little used by God—even if He does bestow His power gifts upon them.*

A COMPLETE TOOL KIT MAY BE A MARVELOUS GIFT FOR A carpenter, but it would be useless without the sweat of his brow. Gifts call for commitment; as Romans 12:7 says, "Let us use it in our ministering." His life is poured out with ours. Gifts are for givers.

To get, give! When Jesus sent out His 12 apostles, He gave them authority to work various miracles and charged them thus: "As you go, proclaim this message: 'The Kingdom of heaven has come near.' Heal the sick, raise the dead, cleanse those who have leprosy, drive out demons. Freely you have received; freely give" (Matthew 10:7, 8 NIV). Jesus clearly emphasized that these gifts have been freely given by Him, and likewise they were to be graciously dispensed. However, the disciples had to expend their energies to do the going, travel across treacherous terrain, sacrifice their comforts and perhaps be persecuted. The gift is free, but walking out the journey that the gift empowers you for, requires something from you.

ASK AND RECEIVE

> *The anointing of Holy Spirit is not for sale, and if it were, no one could afford it. All that is required is that you come and drink freely. "Come, all you who are thirsty, come to the waters; and you who have no money, come, buy and eat! Come, buy wine and milk without money and without cost." (Isaiah 55:1 NIV)*

THE POWER OF THE HOLY SPIRIT CAN'T BE WORKED UP, pulled down, manufactured or generated by hard work and much praying. The Holy Spirit doesn't wait until you sweat. Jesus said, "Ask and it will be given to you...Everyone who asks receives" (Matthew 7:7, 8). God only has gifts; He has nothing for sale. He has no bargains, no discounts, no negotiation, no haggling and no agreements. He is one-sided—He just gives. And we can only do one thing—receive. He wants nothing from us in payment. If you are a dead coal, get the fire of the Holy Spirit and become a living coal. He will get you burning at once.

GOD'S CANDY FOR YOU

> *God has more than enough of everything for all His children and indeed, for all His creation. You do not need to be envious or jealous of another human being. And you do not need to sabotage, slander or malign others to get ahead. If He did not withhold His Son from us (Romans 8:32) and has given us His Spirit freely (1 Corinthians 2:12), what else would He withhold from you?*

IN POST-WAR GERMANY, MY SIBLINGS AND I RECEIVED A PIECE of candy maybe once a year. When my brother Peter had a piece of candy in his mouth, I did NOT try to steal it, but rather did some quick thinking. From whom did my brother get the candy? There was only one possible source—Mother. My mom, I knew, was very fair. She wouldn't give a piece of candy to one of her children if she didn't have one for each of us. I would run to Mom and shout, "Mom, where is MY candy, please?" And there it was...she put it right into my hand. In the same way, if you see God bless a fellow Christian, another church or ministry, don't be jealous! Go to Jesus! He's also got "candy" for you. In Luke 15:31, the Father said to His son, "All that I have is yours." This promise is for us too!

THE GREATER GIFT

"Nevertheless when one turns to the Lord, the veil is taken away. Now the Lord is the Spirit; and where the Spirit of the Lord is, there is liberty. But we all, with unveiled face, beholding as in a mirror the glory of the Lord, are being transformed into the same image from glory to glory, just as by the Spirit of the Lord."

2 CORINTHIANS 3:16-18

HIMSELF – THE GREATER GIFT

> The Holy Spirit should not be confused with His gifts and works. The Holy Spirit is greater than His effect on us or even the world. His presence in our lives is greater than His gifts. The Holy Spirit does not come just so we can speak with tongues, but when He is there, tongues are an evidence. All His gifts are there to foster His relationship with us and with the world.

A BRIDE DOESN'T MARRY THE BRIDEGROOM FOR HIS RING but for him. God is not a show-off. His purpose is always love—to love us, to gain our love and to be with us in dynamic fellowship. He works upon us, through us and with us. He is the strength of our arm and the unquenchable fire in our soul. He brings us spiritual gifts, spiritual fruit and unity (1 Corinthians 12). He first applies the blood of Christ to wipe out the stain of our sin, then brings us to new birth and much more. However, quite apart from what He does, the Spirit comes as Himself, for that is what He is—our great gift. It is the desire for God that makes a true Christian, not merely signs and wonders.

WE ARE NOT SELF-SUFFICIENT

> We are designed to be dependent on the grace and power of God. Apart from Him, we can do nothing (John 15:5). Our sufficiency is of Him (2 Corinthians 3:5). God puts His Spirit in us, because we need Him to comfort, to guide and even to correct us. He activates His gifts and power in us because we need it for His mission—spiritual equipment for a spiritual assignment.

WE ARE NOT SET UP IN BUSINESS ALL ON OUR OWN WITH A lump sum of spiritual capital and power resources making us independent. We are not self-sufficient little "christs." We receive, moment by moment, "out of" Christ's fullness our fullness, like the branches of a vine receive sap. We are not vines unto ourselves, living separate existences, but we are complete in Him (Colossians 2:10).

We are not called to go into the entire world with our own little power plant so that people will think how wonderful we are. We could parade our own charisma and make the sparks fly for an hour; but soon our personal power plant will run out of fuel. We are not generators; we are but conductors of His power. Ephesians 1:22 and 23 describes "...the Church, which is His body, the fullness of Him who fills all in all." He is to fill us and move through us. We are channels not the source. Jesus declared, "As the branch cannot bear fruit of itself, unless it abides in the vine, neither can you, unless you abide in Me" (John 15:4).

NEW LAW OPERATES

Be buoyant in the Spirit. You are designed to float in the waters of the Holy Spirit. Don't resist, don't fight, just relax. Let go, and let the great and glorious currents of the Holy Spirit carry you into your destiny.

ONE DAY, GOD SAID TO ME, "DO YOU KNOW WHAT IT MEANS to swim?" I'm a good swimmer, so I thought I knew. But did I? The Holy Spirit helped me to see something I didn't appreciate before. He said, "When you are swimming, you are in another element, and a new law operates. You must let go and rest fully upon the waters of the river. Those waters carry you." I understood what He was saying. As I swim in the Holy Spirit, His waters carry me. The Spirit lifts me, just as swimming takes the weight off my feet, giving my back a holiday and my joints a vacation. He does the work. What, then, is the real handicap? The real handicap is relying upon yourself. Depend on your own energy and ability, and you will be trudging along the river bank, right beside the very waters which could bear you up and carry you along with minimum effort.

STIRRING UP THE GIFT

"When I call to remembrance the genuine
faith that is in you...Therefore I remind you
to stir up the gift of God which is in you
through the laying on of my hands."

2 TIMOTHY 1:5, 6

SPIRITUALLY ACTIVATED

The gifts of the Spirit are not natural talents. One's natural abilities cannot be called "spiritual gifts." Spiritual gifts are Divinely activated. God can work through anyone. He does not give tongues to linguists only, wisdom only to trained counselors or healing gifts just to doctors. He does not need us to be brilliant to use us.

CREATED IN THE IMAGE OF GOD, MAN IS ENDOWED WITH natural talents that allow him to work, be focused and participate in God's redemptive purpose. But beyond that, God also gives additional gifts through the Holy Spirit to the regenerated man (1 Corinthians 12:1-11). These are not natural talents; they are spiritual gifts that enhance our ability to participate in God's redemptive work. Through the gifts of the Spirit, we can bypass natural excuses, deficiencies and inadequacies. His strength is made perfect in our weaknesses (2 Corinthians 12:9), and we can do all things through Him who strengthens us (Philippians 4:13).

NO MARVELS FOR THE SAKE OF MARVELS

The gifts of the Spirit operate by faith in God not faith in a specific theory. They are not channeled through any doctrine except that of redemption. The Holy Spirit only glorifies the crucified Christ.

GOD GIVES NO MARVELS FOR THE SAKE OF MARVELS. HE IS NOT a showman. He is not in the business of supplying sensations to bring acclaim to any strutting egotist. The Holy Spirit is in league with the crucified Christ—even linked in name, the Spirit of Christ. They have one mind—to defeat the devil through the Gospel. The Spirit finds fulfillment only in the Gospel. The Gospel is so big; it is totally comprehensive, leaving nothing untouched—visible or invisible, in earth, heaven or hell.

NO MEDAL OF HONOR

> *The gifts of the Spirit (1 Corinthians 12:7-11) are not medals of honor to be worn on Sunday morning at church. "I have five, how many do you have?" THEY ARE TOOLS FOR THE JOB and are handed out the moment you report for God's work. He won't give you a hammer when you need a chisel. The Lord will give you daily the perfect tool for the assigned job. If the tools are applied, you will see miracles.*

THE WORD "POWER" IN ACTS 1:8 (*DUNAMIS*), IS POTENTIAL, power in reserve, like a stick of dynamite. It will just lie there, like stone, until activated. People pray for "the power" and no doubt receive it. The *dunamis* potency is directed to human need. We can be like spiritual bodybuilders, developing for the sake of being strong. What is the use of a man being able to lift 500 pounds above his head in a show if he cannot lift a finger to help his wife in the kitchen? What is the use of all our boasts of power if we don't do the jobs that need to be done? The release of the power of the Spirit is never possible until we are active.

FEEDING ON THE WORD

> *Jesus admonishes us not to lay up our treasures on earth, where they are exposed to the elements and vulnerable to thieves, but instead to lay them up in*

heaven, where they are kept secure (Matthew 6:19-21). To that end, we must take heed not to enrich our intellect or emotions at the expense of our spirit.

THE HEATHENS HAD BEEN "CARRIED AWAY" BY THEIR PREVIOUS knowledge, which was similar, but belonged to "dumb idols" (1 Corinthians 12:2). The Greeks were famous for worldly learning, but the things of the Holy Spirit are different. A university doctorate in social sciences or physics does not make us wise in the things of God. These latter are learned by getting fire into one's spirit not just cold facts into one's head. If we want to grow spiritually, we must feed our spirit with the Word of God and pray in the Spirit.

ASSISTANCE FROM THE HOLY SPIRIT

Why always doubt the Word of God? Why not doubt the lies of the devil? Today, choose to doubt your doubts, and decide to believe the Word of God. If you do, you'll soon receive heavenly assistance from the Holy Spirit.

WHY IS IT SO EASY TO BELIEVE THE LIES OF THE DEVIL? WHAT if Eve had chosen to doubt the words of the serpent instead? The outcome would definitely have been different for all of us (Genesis 3). Once you make the decision to trust God more than you trust your doubts, you can access Divine help. Holy Spirit assistance will help to build your faith, and it is faith that moves the mountains which doubt creates.

POWER FROM ON HIGH

"I can do all things through Christ
Who strengthens me."

PHILIPPIANS 4:13

INEXHAUSTIBLE POWER

> *Knowing all about a power station can still leave you in the cold and dark. You can touch the very walls of a nuclear power plant but still be freezing. The key to accessing the available heat is to tap into the power source. There is inexhaustible power of the Holy Spirit on the inside of you to overcome temptation and stay holy, to walk in wisdom and excel in your career, to overcome sicknesses and diseases—if only you will learn to tap into it (2 Peter 1:3).*

THE HOLY SPIRIT LIVES WITHIN US, GIVING US THE POWER TO resist the devil and overcome evil. We must only ask Him to help us. Think of it like this: You have electricity in your home. The house is wired and connected to the power station. If you arrive at home on a dark night, there may be no light or heat in your house. You know what to do. You press the switch, and power comes through. You have light and warmth. Living in the power of the Spirit is like turning the switch on. Everything else is ready. It's only waiting for us.

GOD'S POWER COMES UNFILTERED

> *The power of the Holy Spirit is the real deal—the real Divine power, not a counterfeit or duplicate. God's voice is not muffled in the Scriptures. It speaks with authority and authenticity: "Come to Me all who labor and are heavy laden, and I will give you rest" (Matthew 11:28). The offer is clear and concise; if you receive Christ, you will live a Divine life.*

IN OUR HOMES, POWER DOES NOT COME TO US DIRECT FROM the generators. It is filtered through sub-stations and transformers to reduce the voltage. The power of God, however, does not come to us filtered. When Jesus appears, He is not a pale shadow of what He was—a mere breath. We don't have a phantom Christ; He is the living Jesus not an echo of a faraway hope. The Holy Spirit is bound to honor the Gospel, and through Him, Jesus can step into our midst. You can't bring the Gospel without power any more than having fire without heat. I am not theorizing, but I am talking about my walk with Him. It's real and it works.

NO FADING AWAY

> *The power of God is not an impersonal power that can fade away or drain off. The power of God IS God. Holy Spirit power IS the Holy Spirit. God does not evaporate, fade away, leak or become weaker. Time does not affect God—not even 1,000 years. If you stay connected with God, you will walk in power.*

THE POWER OF GOD IS EVER-STRONG AND ALWAYS AVAILABLE. Paul could tell the Romans a year or two ahead of time that he would come "in the fullness of the blessing of the Gospel of Christ" and that he would "impart to you some spiritual gift" (benefit) to the church (not to an individual) when he came (Romans 15:29; 1:11). He knew the abiding and continuous flow of God's Spirit. The only time Christians need a re-charge is when they have stopped obeying and their contacts with God have become corroded (like with a car battery). Then, they need to clean up their act and start moving again. The power of God comes as you go not as you sit.

NO NEW ANOINTING

> *Once anointed, always anointed. Spring, summer, fall or winter, in the wilderness or the rainforest, alone or with others, the anointing is always*

> *there. You can challenge your greatest enemy, overcome the greatest obstacle and fulfill your God-given destiny; all you have to do is believe.*

DAVID STRIKES ME AS THE ONE MAN IN THE OLD TESTAMENT who knew what it meant to be anointed. He was gripped by the knowledge that God was with him. For example, he went out to challenge Goliath entirely in the assurance of his anointing. He did not ask Samuel to anoint him again, this time with perhaps a "Goliath Anointing." He did not ask the intercessors to pray for him. He did not even pray for himself. He had been anointed and so he remained anointed—the passing of time had changed nothing. He ran toward the Philistine and cried, "You come to me with a shield, with a spear and with a javelin. But I come to you in the name of the Lord of Hosts" (1 Samuel 17:45). And what happened? The teenage David felled the giant.

FIRE POINTS

SECTION 6:

PEOPLE AFLAME–THE HOLY SPIRIT AND THE BELIEVER

NO CARBON COPIES

"We have different gifts, according to the grace given to each of us. If your gift is prophesying, then prophesy in accordance with your faith; if it is serving, then serve; if it is teaching, then teach; if it is to encourage, then give encouragement; if it is giving, then give generously; if it is to lead, do it diligently; if it is to show mercy, do it cheerfully."

ROMANS 12:6-8 NIV

THE SPIRIT OF NEWNESS

> *"See, I am doing a new thing! Now it springs up; do you not perceive it?"* (Isaiah 43:19 NIV). *God's Spirit is at work in us, renewing and refreshing us so that we do not fall back into our old ways or even good traditions. Throughout your life, God wants to do new things, set new records, birth new ideas and work through you to change the world. Don't be stuck in the old; the Spirit of Newness is on you.*

IF I UNDERSTAND GOD AT ALL, HE IS A CREATOR—AN originator. He creates masterpieces every time. He will not even make two snowflakes, two sunsets or two human beings alike. His mind is too fertile and too creative for repetitive work. The word "NEW" is God's own word. The Holy Spirit is the Spirit of newness, bringing constant renewal and constant blossoming: New birth, new tongues, new wine, new songs and a new heart. He brings a new Spirit, a new covenant, a new name, making us a new creation. He has given us a new commandment and made a new heaven and a new earth. Yet it is the same Spirit and the same aim—world salvation. And here is our role, being co-workers together with Christ (1 Corinthians 3:9).

BIG OR SMALL FLAMES

> *You have a Divine DNA. The power you carry is derived from God Himself. It is not inferior or counterfeit; it is the real thing. He Who is in you is far greater and superior than he that is in the world (1 John 4:4). Be bold and courageous!*

AT PENTECOST, WE READ THAT WHEN THE HOLY SPIRIT CAME upon the disciples in the Upper Room, there were "divided tongues, as of fire..." (Acts 2:3). DIVIDED from what? The tongues of flame were divided from the BIG FIRE which is GOD. Little flames broke loose from God and fell, one on each head. The smallest of all flames represents GOD as MUCH AS the biggest.

NO MORE ORDINARY

> *The Divine fire that comes from the baptism of the Holy Spirit changes your status from ordinary to extraordinary. You take on a Divine mandate and assignment so that you no longer live for yourself; you surrender your fears and ambitions and take on a Divine purpose. You become a chosen vessel.*

MOSES HAD SEEN BUSHES AND SHRUBS EVERY DAY FOR 40 years. He did not go around gazing at or studying bushes. Wilderness bushes are not fascinating, cultivated, colorful or blossoming. They are quite unbeautiful. But God took one of them, very ordinary by itself, and made it extraordinary. It burst into flames—but was not consumed (Exodus 3:2). Then He spoke from it—the voice from the burning bush. Moses, in a way, was like the bush—ordinary and even of a lower grade. He was just a piece of driftwood—a fugitive murderer hiding from justice with no future. He was a mere shepherd, and "all shepherds are detestable to the Egyptians" (Genesis 46:34 NIV). Moses saw that bush burning without it turning to ash. He had no idea that this was a life-changing moment. Curious, he turned aside to see it, gazing at it in fascination. Then, a Divine flame leaped from the bush and transferred into his very soul. Moses, a mortal, became a Flame Man. "He makes...His servants flames of fire" (Hebrews 1:7 NIV). On that day, when you turn aside to see the burning bush, you will no longer be ordinary.

YOUR ORIGINAL ANOINTING

> *You are uniquely created, anointed and appointed by God for His purposes and for your time and season. "As your days, so shall your strength be" (Deuteronomy 33:25). Instead of worrying about what you do not have, focus on what you do have, step out in faith and watch God work through you.*

ON THE DAY OF PENTECOST, THE 120 DID NOT CRY FOR A double anointing. Please note: NOBODY LEFT THE UPPER ROOM WITH TWO FLAMES ON THEIR HEAD. Just "one sat upon each of them" (Acts 2:3). But this one flame represents the whole fire of God—its authority, power and glory. When I travel the world, I am often asked, "Please pray for me; I want your anointing." My counter-question? "Do you think that if I give you my anointing, I will go home without? Surely not." But here is a wonderful secret: If you got Reinhard Bonnke's anointing, you would become a copy of Bonnke. And let me tell you: I personally do not want to be a copy from a copy—and God doesn't want that for you either.

If you want to know something about the character of God, just consider nature. Over 7.5 billion human beings do not have the same fingerprints, and no two leaves of any tree have the same structure. Why? Because God is not a duplicator—He is the Creator. He only produces ORIGINALS and operates no duplicating machine. Your flame on your head is so personal that it bears your name. It is custom-made for you only. It would not fit anybody else. Nobody on earth can serve God exactly as you! You are unique—and so is your anointing!

MORE THAN A
DOUBLE PORTION

"Most assuredly, I say to you, he who believes in
Me, the works that I do he will do also; and greater
works than these he will do, because I go to My
Father. And whatever you ask in My name, that
I will do, that the Father may be glorified in the
Son. If you ask anything in My name, I will do it."

JOHN 14:12-14

THE FINGER OF GOD

> *There is a finger on you, but it is not a finger of destruction. It is the Finger of God, pointed directly at you to bless you, distinguish you and empower you for His service—to heal the sick, raise the dead and cast out devils! The finger of God is the Holy Spirit (Acts 10:38). He delivers you from every power of darkness and releases God's goodness in your life.*

ISRAEL'S BLESSINGS ARE COVENANTED TO THE "COMMONWEALTH of Israel" (Ephesians 2:12). Christ Jesus linked wonders to the new Christian Commonwealth: "If I cast out demons by the finger of God, surely the Kingdom of God has come upon you" (Luke 11:20). There is no power greater than that of the Holy Spirit. It is Kingdom power, and no other power matches it. By the Spirit, He distributes His ministries to whom He chooses.

ELIJAH'S MANTLE

> *Jesus said, "Behold, a greater than Solomon is here" (Matthew 12:42 KJV), "Before Abraham was, I Am" (John 8:58), and concerning John the Baptist, "If you are willing to receive it, he is Elijah who is to come" (Matthew 11:14). It is important to realize that you have received a mantle far superior to Elijah's—Jesus' mantle, the baptism of the Holy Spirit.*

IT IS NOT UNCOMMON IN PENTECOSTAL-CHARISMATIC CIRCLES to hear people praying for Elijah's mantle: the power to call down fire and work miracles, signs and wonders as Elijah did. However, Jesus makes it clear, "And these signs will follow those who believe: In My name they will cast out demons; they will speak with new tongues;

they will take up serpents; and if they drink anything deadly, it will by no means hurt them; they will lay hands on the sick, and they will recover" (Mark 16:17, 18). Need we pray for Elijah's mantle? No, I don't believe so. Jesus gives us His mantle, the baptism in the Holy Spirit. All we must do is believe and walk in it, and signs and wonders will follow.

THE UNTHINKABLE

The Lord God is not only "in our midst," but He is within us. His absence is unthinkable. He does not have to be sought, fasted and clamored for, or "claimed." His presence is essential to the very nature of the Christian faith.

THE PROPHETS PREDICTED IT, BUT THEY THEMSELVES NEVER knew it. The last of the prophets, John the Baptist, said, "I baptize you with water...but He will baptize you in the Holy Spirit and fire" (Matthew 3:11). As part of the redemptive package, New Testament believers enjoy a new depth of Divine intimacy. Beyond fellowshipping with God, He is within us, in each and every individual saved by His grace (John 14:17). We don't have to earn it; His love guarantees it. If we are born again, cleansed by the blood of the Lamb of God from our sins, there is nothing we need to do about His presence; He is already there anyway and always! That is the glory of our faith.

HE DWELLS WITH US

God is near night and day. If He waits in church while we get on with life, how then would He save us and be our strength? Pagans go to the shrines of their gods, but Christ is with us always. He is with me now, as I write at this desk, as well as when I am preaching in crusades. We vary, but He does not (James 1:17). Opportunity does not dictate to Him. He has no moods and is not manipulated by our moods. He doesn't come and go, chased back and forth by our attitudes. We are temperamental, but He is forever the same.

GOD DOESN'T JUST TAKE ADVANTAGE OF THE CHANCE moment when we are in a spiritual frame of mind. Wherever we are, He is there—even when we are asleep and unconscious of His nearness. Psalm 4:8 declares, "I will both lie down in peace and sleep; for You, O Lord, make me dwell in safety." We can "dwell" in safety because He "dwells" with us. Christ said "Lo, I am with you always, even to the end of the age" (Matthew 28:20).

ROYAL PRIESTHOOD

But you are a chosen generation, a royal priesthood,
a holy nation, His own special people, that you
may proclaim the praises of Him who called
you out of darkness into His marvelous light.

1 PETER 2:9

FIRE-CROWNED HEADS

> *You are a crown prince(ss). God has crowned you with glory and fire. You wield authority and power on your head—the tongues of fire of the Holy Spirit. "Behold, I give unto you power and authority to tread on scorpions and serpents and over all the power of the enemy..." (Luke 10:19). You are not a wimp. Don't cower before the enemy, and don't live an ordinary life.*

YOU ARE MADE TO WEAR A FIRE-WREATH, OR A FIRE-CROWN! That was no committee-decision. It is God's will that every believer be carrying the flame, wearing a monarch's DIADEM of Holy Spirit power. A noble WREATH OF FIRE on our heads. DIVINE RECOGNITION. A CROWN OF LIVING AUTHORITY. Baptized in the Spirit—CROWNED WITH POWER.

As Moses blessed the Israelites, his words about Joseph were more than beautiful poetry (Deuteronomy 33:13-17). It spoke a prophetic promise: "May the favor of Him who dwelt in the burning bush rest on the head of Joseph, on the brow of the prince among his brothers." The favor of Him that dwelt in the burning bush crowning Joseph is a Bible promise to us. When the God of the burning bush crowns us, that crown brings us spiritual majesty and authority. We speak with power and assurance because we KNOW by Whose authority we speak.

HEAD HIGH

> *The Gospel was not given to level us all to the lowest common denominator, but to create new creatures and to give to all of us the dignity of the sons of God! Men who once were savages are reclaimed and walk now as princes. Hallelujah! What a reason to preach the Gospel! Could anything be more thrilling, adventurous and worthwhile? What else is worth life's effort?*

BELIEVERS CAN WALK THROUGH THIS WORLD WITH HEADS held high, carrying the dignity of the family of God as lords and ladies of the kingdom of heaven. "Let the weak say, 'I am strong'" (Joel 3:10). We are the precious and costly purchase of the Redeemer. God is with us. We have been endued with the power of the Almighty, cherished by angels, girdled with strength, guided by an all-wise call, involved in the Creator's eternal orders and perfumed by grace. The Gospel brings God and us together forever!

LIVING FIRE

> *It is surprising which people God uses. Not often does He use the great men of earth, brilliant leaders or celebrities, but He usually chooses men with no great achievements in the world. God does not use many crowned heads of state. He chooses the fire-crowned. That is the qualification for His work—the authority of faith and fire.*

THERE WERE MANY AVAILABLE CAESARS AND RULERS: PILATE, Caiaphas the High priest, the religious and political elite of their day. But Jesus bypassed them all and went to lowly fishermen and tax collectors—the uneducated, uncultured traders by the sea of Galilee. Some had cheated and one had stolen, but because they were pliable and yielding, He could shape them into world changers, and He did. To this day, Jesus is still doing the same—using men and women from all backgrounds. He cleanses them with His blood, empowers them by His Spirit and uses them as world changers. You can be one of them too: living fire.

NEW DIMENSIONS OF GLORY AND POWER

"Now Peter and John went up together to the temple at the hour of prayer, the ninth hour. And a certain man lame from his mother's womb was carried, whom they laid daily at the gate of the temple which is called Beautiful, to ask alms from those who entered the temple; who, seeing Peter and John about to go into the temple, asked for alms. And fixing his eyes on him, with John, Peter said, 'Look at us.' So he gave them his attention, expecting to receive something from them. Then Peter said, 'Silver and gold I do not have, but what I do have I give you: In the name of Jesus Christ of Nazareth, rise up and walk.' And he took him by the right hand and lifted him up, and immediately his feet and ankle bones received strength. So he, leaping up, stood and walked and entered the temple with them—walking, leaping, and praising God. And all the people saw him walking and praising God. Then they knew that it was he who sat begging alms at the Beautiful Gate of the temple; and they were filled with wonder and amazement at what had happened to him."

ACTS 3:1-10

A NEW DIMENSION

> *The baptism in the Spirit with speaking in tongues is no new Reformation, no renovation or decoration. It is liberation and gives Christian teaching a new dimension. The baptism in the Spirit is simply typical of Who the Holy Spirit is—causing us to be "endued" with power.*

THE PROPHETS OF OLD WERE NOT BAPTIZED IN THE SPIRIT, but they were moved when the Spirit came upon them. It marked them as prophets. Miracles also sometimes took place. When these supernatural effects were seen, they were put down to the breath of God. The word breath is the same as Spirit in Hebrew (*ruah*). When King Saul was touched by God, everybody could see it. They said that the breath or Spirit of God had come upon Him. He did not indwell people in the Old Testament, but rather moved them from time to time for special purposes. Under the new covenant, the Holy Spirit indwells the believer and empowers him, making the New Testament experience much better than the Old Testament.

TREASURES IN EARTHEN VESSELS

> *The Holy Spirit in us is treasure, but we are not like a treasure chest carrying trinkets and ornaments locked up in a shipwreck on the ocean floor—rusty, cold and dormant. We are vessels carrying pure, hot, liquid gold. It is impossible to touch us or gaze upon us and not feel the heat.*

WHO ARE THE MOST RIDICULOUS—THE PEOPLE DANCING FOR joy with the vision of God or the people posing unperturbed like the Sphinx, which was unmoved even when Napoleon fired a cannon at it? Flesh and blood are not granite that should experience the Spirit and show no sign of it. What we have in earthen vessels is "treasure," to show that this all-surpassing power is from God (2 Corinthians 4:7). Something totally strange will be evident to minds alienated from God, like Festus said to Paul, "You are beside yourself. Much learning is driving you mad!" (Acts 26:24). How else could it be today when people experience the original brand of Christianity?

MORE THAN CAPABLE

"If God is for us, who can be against us? He who did not spare His own Son, but delivered Him up for us all, how shall He not with Him also freely give us all things?...Who shall separate us from the love of Christ? Shall tribulation, or distress, or persecution, or famine, or nakedness, or peril, or sword?...Yet in all these things we are more than conquerors through Him who loved us. For I am persuaded that neither death nor life, nor angels nor principalities nor powers, nor things present nor things to come, nor height nor depth, nor any other created thing, shall be able to separate us from the love of God which is in Christ Jesus our Lord."

ROMANS 8:31-32, 35, 37-39

DESIGNED FOR RUGGED TERRAIN

> The Christian is not a weakling—a fragile species subject to the harshness
> of the elements and the brutalities of others. Like Esther, the most well-bred,
> royal and dainty of us is not to be trifled with (Esther 7:3-10). The power
> of the Holy Spirit makes us as bold as a lion (Proverbs 28:1). We roar
> as of the Lion of the tribe Judah, and why not? We are sons and daughters
> of God!

WHEN THE HOLY SPIRIT CAME UPON THE BELIEVERS, IT GAVE
them more than the power to work miracles, signs and wonders.
It also toughened them up for the challenges of the times and the
persecutions they would face. With the coming of the Holy Spirit, the
apostles discovered a new resilience, a new strength within them and
a power that operated in their weakness, sending them out into a
brutalized, pagan world to demolish its idol establishment and change
history. That is a true mark of "the Spirit-filled life."

PERPETUAL SPRINGTIME

> The Spirit-filled life is not an experience to be cultivated in special conditions,
> like indoor lilies. Christians are not flowers. The Holy Spirit makes believers
> tough specimens for all conditions. They carry perpetual springtime in their
> soul and are "winterized."

YOU ARE NOT LIKE A PLANT CULTIVATED IN A GREEN HOUSE,
only able to survive under special conditions and incapable of
surviving on your own. The believer is planted by springs of living
water. You carry a perpetual springtime; your leaves will not wither,

no matter the external conditions or environment. Regardless of the circumstances, you will bear fruit for God (Psalm 1).

FIREPLACE

> *Without a fireplace, the nicest home can feel unwelcome in a cold winter. Like a stove, you are designed to bring warmth and comfort to a cold, dark and ugly world. Let the wind of the Spirit of God blow on your embers, blowing away the dust of unbelief and hopelessness. As you add logs of faith in the Word of God to your little fireplace, you will begin blazing hot with the fire of the Holy Spirit.*

GOD CREATED THE HUMAN HEART TO BE A FIREPLACE. THE "mighty, rushing wind" had to come first to blow out all ash and trash, and then the fire followed (Acts 2:1-4). Real fire radiates heat. Fish has the same temperature as the water in which it swims, and some Christians are just like that. They have the temperature of godless entertainment and wonder what is wrong. When our fire grate is filled with fire, we are hot. We change the temperature of our surroundings.

FIRE SOLVES PROBLEMS

> *The devil is comfortable where people are spiritually cold; he remains comfortable regardless of how religious they are. Get ablaze with the fire of the Holy Spirit, and the heat will drive the enemy away.*

A LADY SAID TO ME "I HAVE A DEMON SITTING ON MY HEAD."
"Are you a child of God?" I asked. She nodded. I was amazed. Suddenly, the Holy Spirit spoke to me and I asked her, "Do you know that flies love to sit on a cold stove, often for a long time? Get the fire and heat of the Holy Spirit into your life, and your devil-problem is solved forever." When your "stove" is hot and some fly approaches, it suddenly senses the heat and sharply veers away. Praise God, we are protected by "a wall of fire"—the fire of the Holy Spirit.

NEVER ALONE

"But now, thus says the Lord, Who created you, O Jacob, and He Who formed you, O Israel: 'Fear not, for I have redeemed you; I have called you by your name; you are Mine. When you pass through the waters, I will be with you; and through the rivers, they shall not overflow you. When you walk through the fire, you shall not be burned, nor shall the flame scorch you. For I am the Lord your God, the Holy One of Israel, your Savior...'"

ISAIAH 43:1-3

CONSTANCY IS THE GUARANTEE

> *God did not give His presence to us as a group. No, the gift of His presence, of His Holy Spirit, is personal. It is for you. It is for me. It is for each one of us individually.*

GOD SAID, "AS I WAS WITH MOSES, SO I WILL BE WITH YOU" (Joshua 1:5). We read, "The Lord was with Joseph" (Genesis 39:2). This individual assurance embraced all of Israel forever. He told these leaders that He would not fail them, and that promise was for the entire nation. We read the promise of His nearness in Scripture, written long ago to all believers, but it should not to be watered down to some vague sentiment. It is a personal guarantee to me, to you and to every reader of the Bible.

MORE OF GOD?

> *You have the full Holy Spirit, in person and in power—not a partial Holy Spirit. He is not present in bits and pieces. You don't need more of God. You have all of Him and His fullness. Just surrender to Him, believe that He is truly all there and you will see amazing manifestations of the Holy Spirit in your life.*

MORE OF GOD? PLEASE TAKE NOTE: IF WE ARE IN THE OCEAN, we are wet and cannot get wetter. We are wet with the whole Pacific, the whole Atlantic of the Spirit, not dampened by a drop from a child's seaside bucket. The wetness, the water that clings to us, stretches to the shoreless reaches of God. We are one in the Spirit with all who bathe in those waters. Think about it. Apostle Paul said, "For we were all baptized by one Spirit so as to form one body...and we were all given the one Spirit to drink" (1 Corinthians 12:13). The spiritual sign is fire—fervency. The physical sign is speaking with tongues.

DOUBLE SAFTEY

> *The Father joins with the Son to ensure we are cared for. "Your life is hidden with Christ in God" (Colossians 3:3). I like to think of it as a locked safe in a strong-room. We are in double safety. Nothing can separate us.*

I LIVE WITH THE ASSURANCE THAT I AM WASHED IN THE BLOOD of Jesus, and nobody can pluck me from His hand (John 10:28-30). Satan cannot kidnap my soul. It is hidden with Christ in God, and it bears the seal-mark of the blood of Christ (1 Peter 1:18, 19). "Rejoice...again I will say rejoice!" (Philippians 4:4).

PRAYER CORRECTION

> *Let this truth sink deep into your soul. Let it reflect in your life—in everything you do or wherever you go. The Lord is with you. He will never leave you nor forsake you (Hebrews 13:5). This is not a cliché or charismatic jargon. It is a spiritual truth and reality.*

WE HAVE THE HABIT OF PRAYING, AS I USED TO WHEN I WAS A young man, "Please, Lord Jesus, come into our midst." One day, I woke up and said, "How can I plead with someone to come who promised to never leave me?" This is true of Jesus, Who promised to never, ever leave us (Matt 28:20). We need to live in the reality of His constant presence and change our old style of prayer.

FIRE POINTS

SECTION 7:

A FOREST OF FIRE–THE HOLY SPIRIT AND THE CHURCH

A NEW GENESIS

"Then those who gladly received his (Peter's) word were baptized; and that day about three thousand souls were added to them. And they continued steadfastly in the apostles' doctrine and fellowship, in the breaking of bread, and in prayers. Then fear came upon every soul, and many wonders and signs were done through the apostles."

ACTS 2:41-43

WHAT A GIFT!

> *"And suddenly there came a sound from heaven, as of a rushing, mighty wind..." (Acts 2:2). The Holy Spirit came with great force and a demonstration of power. The Church thrives when it ministers in this power, and the gates of hell cannot prevail against it.*

WHEN YOU GRASP THE FULL IMPORT OF WHAT IT MEANS TO have the Holy Spirit baptism, you will become another person. You will join the army standing with the battering ram of the Word of the Cross that will pulverize the strongholds of the devil. This is the drum-roll thunder of God's invincible army on the march. When God filled me with His Spirit and opened my lips to speak with tongues, He opened my ears to hear the triumphant peal of the trumpet announcing that Jesus has all power in heaven and on earth. What a gift!

THE FIRST CHRISTIAN CONGREGATION

> *The first Christian congregation was solemn but not a quiet gathering or a powerless bunch. There was prophesying, there was preaching, and there were salvations and baptisms. The Spirit of God began to move in a mighty way and has not stopped since.*

TO TALK ABOUT HIM, WE HAVE FIRST TO IDENTIFY HIM. HE IS the power of Pentecost. He began the Christian Church. We can pinpoint when and where this happened. It was in AD 29 at the annual Jewish festival held 50 days after Christ's crucifixion, called the Day of Pentecost. That morning, the Spirit of God burst upon the world, not as a sweet influence but literally as a hurricane (Acts 2:1-4). He announced His own arrival with the miracle of 120 disciples empowered and speaking in tongues. This noisy outburst attracted the first Christian congregation.

PERMANENCE

You cannot shake the Holy Spirit free from the Church. The Holy Spirit abides; He has come to stay. That is His job—His assignment. He is with us always even to the uttermost bounds of the earth (Acts 1:8). He is with us to empower, encourage and guide us. We do not receive a little bit of the Holy Spirit, to last us for a while, and then have to return for a further supply, like making regular trips to the supermarket. We are always full.

THE DISCIPLES NEVER RETURNED TO THE UPPER ROOM FOR A REPEAT-EXPERIENCE. Jesus told the disciples He was going, but He would send the Comforter who would never go away. Jesus had to leave, but nothing could make the Holy Spirit be absent. Permanence is the essential character of the Spirit. The Spirit ABIDES. First John 2:27 says the anointing "abides." The word "abide" (in Greek *meno*) is a favorite expression of John. It is used 120 times in the New Testament and 63 of them are by John—38 in his Gospel and 25 times in the Epistles. This is only one way that John underlines the continuity of the blessing, power and anointing of God. He has other ways also. He avoids words which suggest an ending in the past, a finish or interruption of the activity of God. He always presents the work of God as on-going.

HOMELESS

> *Without the Church, the Holy Spirit is homeless. He is like Noah's dove that found no resting place away from the ark. Without the Spirit of God, the Church is a mausoleum. But with the Holy Spirit, the church becomes a mighty fortress. Then, we conquer and are not conquered.*

"JESUS REPLIED, 'FOXES HAVE DENS AND BIRDS HAVE NESTS, but the Son of Man has no place to lay his head'" (Matthew 8:20). When Jesus was on earth, He was a man on a mission and had no claim to a home. But through the Holy Spirit, He comes to abide with us (John 14:23). Willing hearts and minds give God more than a platform to execute His purpose; they give the Holy Spirit a home here on earth. God desires to make a home in your life. As it is in heaven, so should it be in your life (Matthew 6:9-13). God wants your life to be a place of comfort, joy, peace and happiness.

THE UNCHANGING TRANSFORMER

"Now when they saw the boldness of Peter and John, and perceived that they were uneducated and untrained men, they marveled. And they realized that they had been with Jesus."

ACTS 4:13

MEN AND WOMEN OF LIKE PASSION

> *Abraham, Moses, Joshua, Deborah, Elijah and Elisha—all these names inspire awe and wonder, but they were people of like passions like you and I (James 5:17). The same Spirit that was upon them is in us. We did not receive a second-rate Spirit or experience, and we should not expect a second-rate result.*

THE BAPTISM IN THE SPIRIT ENDUES BELIEVERS WITH THE Spirit of the prophets. When the prophets experienced God supernaturally, they called it the Spirit of the prophets. Joel 2:28 promised that the same Spirit of the prophets would be poured out on all flesh. People of all kinds would prophesy—not just an individual here and there. Furthermore, this outpouring would not be for a single task but as a permanent gift in Christ to everyone. On the Day of Pentecost, as described in Acts, "a sound like the blowing of a violent wind filled the whole house where they were sitting...and tongues of fire came to rest on each of them." They all spoke with new tongues about the "wonderful works of God." Joel's prophecy was that young and old would prophesy, and Peter declared, "This is what was spoken by the prophet Joel." He described new tongues as prophecy (Acts 2:15-17). Prophecy is utterance under the power of God, and we see it in these last days as we are endued with the same Spirit as the prophets of old.

TRANSFORMATIONAL POWER

> *The transformational power of the Holy Spirit is undisputable. Fishermen and peasants turned into great apostles—weak and indecisive but having become strong and influential. They became spearheads in the Kingdom of God blazing away in the darkness of the world with the fire of the Gospel.*

YOU WOULD THINK IT WAS MISSION IMPOSSIBLE: A GROUP of fishermen charged with changing the world. However, these mostly unlearned nobodies advanced with a new secret. God personally worked with them through signs and wonders. More than that, He barbed their simple words with conviction and guided those words to the hearts of hearers as unerringly and powerfully as David's stone to the head of Goliath. Without personal charisma, the charisma of the Spirit of God endued them. Their "secret" was simple—the Holy Spirit.

FOR THE BEST AND FOR THE WORST OF US

> *The Holy Spirit does not choose the strong and the capable, although He does not ignore them either. However, His main purpose is to give strength to the weak and needy. Their weakness attracts His power, His all-sufficiency and His life-giving dynamism. He comes for the best and for the worst of us, as the Father's Promise sent by the Son. Look at the story of Peter the Apostle:*

PETER DENIED JESUS THREE TIMES WHILE AT THE FIRE ON THE night Jesus was arrested (Mark 14:66-72). Questions as to his identity came to him like a shot, and he miserably denied Jesus his Lord. Tears dripped down his rugged beard, and when Jesus silently looked at him, the melt-down of repentance began. But look what happened to Peter on the Day of Pentecost. He became the spokesman of the Apostles of the Lamb and he also led 3,000 people to the Lord that day (Acts 2). God gives such empowerment to the most miserable people.

GIFTED CHURCH

"There are diversities of gifts, but the same Spirit. There are differences of ministries, but the same Lord. And there are diversities of activities, but it is the same God who works all in all. But the manifestation of the Spirit is given to each one for the profit of all...For as the body is one and has many members, but all the members of that one body, being many, are one body, so also is Christ...Now you are the Body of Christ and members individually."

1 CORINTHIANS 12:4-7, 12, 27

BURNING BUSH

> *Even in the loneliest and driest of deserts the burning bush is magnificent—filled with power and offering hope. God planned our churches to be burning bushes from which He will speak. Seeing a burning bush, church people will hear and will listen to God's voice. We want forests of burning bushes.*

WE ARE BUSHES THAT BURN WITH THE GLORY OF GOD AND the fire of the Holy Spirit, not old reeds in a dirty swamp that are weak, wet and cannot burn. When Moses encountered the burning bush, his life was transformed. This hopeless, wandering, purposeless man received a Divine purpose from God that would change his life, destiny and people. A man who was hiding from the law was empowered to go back with a staff of righteousness to liberate those in captivity. God intends for our churches to be burning bushes from which He will speak and transform the lives of many who are destitute, hopeless, forgotten and abandoned, to give them purpose and a reason to live.

POWER HOUSE OF PRAYER

> *Secret prayer is the secret of power. A prayer room is a power house of the Spirit. But God wants more. He wants His house to be a house of prayer for all nations (Isaiah 56:7). Let prayer go forth to and for the nations, and let the healing waters flood the earth.*

JESUS SAID, "WHEN YOU PRAY, GO INTO YOUR ROOM, CLOSE the door and pray to your Father, who is unseen" (Matthew 6:6 NIV). Close the door of your prayer room, and the door of heaven opens. When the disciples were in the Upper Room, the windows of glory unlocked, and the Holy Spirit rained upon them (Acts 2). The devil will try to stop you from praying, because prayer stops him. All around the world, there are prayer rooms—upper rooms—in churches, colleges and even in administrative offices. They are typical places full of the Gospel and Spirit-filled Christians. A prayer room is a power house. Today, "Pray without ceasing" (1 Thessalonians 5:17).

WHAT THE CHURCH IS NOT

Far in front of all the phenomena of signs and wonders, new tongues, or healings is the preaching and teaching of the Word of God. Miracles are the support system of the truth.

THE PRIMARY AIM OF EVERY CHURCH SERVICE SHOULD BE evangelistic. Why shouldn't every service be open to outsiders? Especially at Holy Communion when the emblems of bread and wine are taken. What a prime opportunity to first preach salvation. That cup of red wine is the greatest preacher in the world, to convict sinners of their sin. It is the Gospel in a cup—an opportunity to invite lost sinners to accept the sacrifice of the Cross. Shall only the clean come to the fountain?

THE GIFTS OF THE SPIRIT ARE
FOR HIS PURPOSES ONLY

The gifts of the Spirit have not been given to us so we can play power games. God's power shapes and forms us as creatures of HIS purposes not OUR purposes. *"Thou hast created all things and for thy pleasure they are and were created" (Revelation 4:11 KJV). What an honor to be called to help build God's eternal Kingdom! Our mortal hands can build His eternal Kingdom here on earth. There is nothing greater.*

THE DESIRE FOR POSITION AND POWER IN THE KINGDOM HAS been seen from the very beginning of the Church. James and John, two of the 12 disciples, asked Jesus, "Grant us that we may sit, one on Your right hand and the other on Your left, in Your glory" (Mark 10:37). But Jesus' response was polite but strong—even if you can drink from My cup, and you usually will, this request is not Mine to grant (Mark 10:39, 40). Throughout history, there have been power struggles, politics and turf wars. Believers have fought for position in the Church, wanting to build their own kingdoms and pursue their own agenda. But there is only one thing that matters—the purpose of God. I hope you and I can dedicate ourselves, our talent and our ambition to building the Kingdom of God. After all, "We are His workmanship, created in Christ Jesus for good works..." (Ephesians 2:10).

THE HOLY SPIRIT IS A COMPOSER

No two persons operate in the Holy Spirit the same way. Neither are any two churches the same. Unity does not mean uniformity and oneness does not mean sameness.

BEING DIFFERENT IS NO SIN. THE EXPRESSION "THE PROFIT OF all" in 1 Corinthians 12:7 is the Greek word *sympheron,* from which comes the English word "symphony." The Holy Spirit is a Composer conducting His own work, bringing counterpoint and harmony from many interlocking themes and instruments. He doesn't need or want everyone playing the same tune. "There are diversities of gifts, but the same Spirit. There are differences of ministries, but the same Lord. And there are diversities of activities, but it is the same God who works all in all" (1 Corinthians 12:4-6).

HOLY SPIRIT-POWERED

"For I determined not to know anything among you except Jesus Christ and Him crucified. I was with you in weakness, in fear, and in much trembling. And my speech and my preaching were not with persuasive words of human wisdom, but in demonstration of the Spirit and of power, that your faith should not be in the wisdom of men but in the power of God."

1 CORINTHIANS 2:2-5

FULL OF PASSION

> *Christians were never intended to fight the world, the flesh and the devil with
> only their natural resources or intellect—whether they lived in the first or the
> 21st century. The Gospel is the "power of God" (Romans 1:16). The Holy
> Spirit gives us the power we need, but not when we ignore Him.*

HOW MUCH PREACHING TODAY SOUNDS AS IF THE PREACHER just returned from the Upper Room with the apostles? How much sounds as if the Gospel is actually the power of God? Preachers often talk to their congregations like doctors—passionless, giving the Holy Spirit no chance to move. The Christian mandate cannot be accomplished without the Spirit's anointing. "Be filled with the Spirit!" is our instruction (Ephesians 5:18). Being purpose-driven is part of it, but being Spirit-driven is the New Testament pattern. He is the motivator and the motivating power.

"THEY CONTINUED"

> *If we want New Testament conditions, we need to study the New Testament
> pattern so we know what to expect. If we do what the apostles did, we get
> what the apostles got. If we preach the original Gospel, we will get the original
> results.*

"AND THEY CONTINUED STEADFASTLY IN THE APOSTLES' doctrine and fellowship, in the breaking of bread, and in prayers. Then fear came upon every soul, and many wonders and signs were done through the apostles...And the Lord added to the Church daily those who were being saved" (Acts 2:42, 43, 47). People pray, "Do it again,

Lord." But we should do *again* what the Early Church Christians did; they were unceasing in their witness (Acts 5:42). They preached, witnessed and worked as if it all depended on them, but then they prayed as if it all depended on God. They depended on God, and God depended on them. Oh, that God can depend on you and me to continue—to be faithful in preaching, in teaching and in witnessing.

LIMITLESS JESUS
UNLIMITED MIRACLES

> *Proclamation comes before confirmation. Preach a limited Jesus, and He cannot be Himself. He does not save unless you preach a Savior. He does not heal unless you preach the Healer. He will bless if you preach the One Who blesses. The Holy Spirit confirms the Word of God (Mark 16:20). He does not confirm our personality, or ego.*

THE HOLY SPIRIT CAN ONLY BLESS WHAT YOU SAY ABOUT Jesus. The Spirit cannot bless what you do not say about Him. If "this same Jesus," the very "Jesus whom Paul preaches," is preached now, the Spirit of God will confirm it (Acts 1:11; 19:13). How many are guilty of stripping our precious Lord? Men stripped Him once for His crucifixion; unbelief strips Him again of His power. He is no longer mighty to save and heal in many churches. To use Paul's expression, He is "restricted" in our lives, which means "hemmed in with no room to work" (2 Corinthians 6:12), caught in cold, crusted unbelief. Again we read in Mark 16:20, "And they went out and preached everywhere, the Lord working with them and confirming the Word through the accompanying signs." They preached, and the Lord confirmed. Proclamation comes before confirmation.

HIS ABIDING PRESENCE

"Be strong and of good courage, do not fear
nor be afraid of them; for the Lord your
God, He is the One Who goes with you.
He will not leave you nor forsake you."

DEUTERONOMY 31:6

"IMMANUEL, GOD WITH US"

> *God's presence does not fluctuate, coming and going. Nothing in the New Testament suggests this. The whole emphasis is on His unfailing presence. Even God's name is given as "Yahweh Shammah," the LORD is there (Ezekiel 48:35). God is with us as He has always been and will always be.*

PROPHESYING THE BIRTH OF JESUS, THE BIBLE USES THE name "Immanuel, God with us" (Matthew 1:23). Scripture gives us many explicit assurances of the Divine presence. God will never leave us alone. "Yea, though I walk through the valley of the shadow of death, I will fear no evil; for You are with me..." (Psalm 23:4). "The Lord will not forsake His people for His great name's sake: because it has pleased the LORD to make you His people" (1 Samuel 12:22). The LORD told Moses, "I will certainly be with you," and to Joshua He said, "As I was with Moses, so I will be with you. I will not leave you nor forsake you" (Exodus 3:12; Joshua 1:5). Psalm 146:6 declares, "He remains faithful forever." The Lord is faithful to us.

FELLOWSHIP WITH GOD

> *We are special—given the opportunity for an intimate, personal relationship with the Creator and Lord of the heavens and the earth. Through the Holy Spirit we fellowship with the Father and His Son Jesus Christ. This is the blessedness of the Christian faith. No other deity or god offers such closeness. We are loved!*

JESUS PROMISED HE WOULD ALWAYS BE WITH US! WHAT manner of man is this? His presence is fellowship. Theologians use the words "Divine immanence." That is not what Jesus promised. "Immanence" means God pervading the world. The atmosphere pervades the planet, but God is not an atmosphere. The Bible speaks of fellowship with Him. We can't have fellowship with an atmosphere. Christians have a Communion Service. In it, we partake of His life. This is an example of the wonderful personal intimacy between the Creator and His creatures. This is the exclusive hallmark of the Lord of heaven and earth. That is impossible for anyone except the one true God, and there is nobody beside Him. That is the special thing about God. He is near to each and everyone (Hebrews 13:5).

"THERE I AM"

> *God is not present in a general sense—for everybody together and yet for nobody in particular. He is not divided in proportion to individuals. His presence is not regulated by our importance. He is fully with each one of us, and that is how He is with the whole gathering. We do not generate or attract His presence. He already is. "I AM."*

CHRIST'S WORDS WERE, "WHERE TWO OR THREE ARE gathered in My name, there I am" (Matthew 18:20). He did not say 'I will come,' but 'there I AM.' How He pre-empts our gatherings is part of the glorious mystery of our God. We don't create or attract His presence by meeting with one another. He doesn't come because we are there. WE come because He is there. "Unto Him shall the gathering of the people be" (Genesis 49:10 KJV). The 'two or three' could be any two or three meeting in His name—believers. It can be within a family—even a husband and wife. He does not withdraw from the domestic circle. Family concerns are His concerns. Christ first came to us in a home—that of Mary and Joseph.

FULLY THERE

God is with us in His fullness, not in percentages. The Spirit of God does not withdraw or retract, evaporate, diminish or leak away. He abides (I John 4:15). God has not covenanted to be with us sometimes, but always.

THE SPIRIT OF GOD DOES NOT JUST TURN UP, LIKE THE congregation on Sundays. He does not wait until we have prepared for His visit with suitable songs. We do not need to pray for God to be there, because He is there—ALWAYS. He is fully there! He would never make His redeeming work dependent on our emotional state, which goes up and down like an elevator in the Empire State building—one moment on the ground floor and the next in the clouds. God's sun never sets; He is always at the highpoint, in noon position.

ACTIVE AND NOT PASSIVE PRESENCE

The Lord's presence is ACTIVE and not passive. He is not with us like a shadow—mute, void of all power, forgettable and contributing nothing to our existence. He is like the Sun, from which we can't and dare not escape, whose power and radiance brings life to our very existence.

WHEN THE SPIRIT OF GOD COMES UPON YOU, THERE IS evidence of a changed life and a constantly changing life from glory to glory (2 Corinthians 3:18). Your life can't stay stagnant; that is adverse to the very nature of God. The Lord of the winds will calm the storms. The Prince of Peace will bring peace into your life. He will heal your body, bless the works of your hand, bless the fruit of your womb and transform you into a living witness. The presence of God is discernible; it has definite impact. The LORD said, "I will certainly be with you," and Jesus said, "I am with you always, even to the end of the age" (Exodus 3:12; Matthew 28:20). Jesus kept His promise. "The disciples went out and preached EVERYWHERE and the Lord worked with them..." (Mark 16:20 NIV).

FIRE POINTS

SECTION 8:

FIRED UP–THE HOLY SPIRIT'S CHALLENGE

IT IS YOUR TIME

"For the promise is to you and to your children, and to all who are afar off, as many as the Lord our God will call."

ACTS 2:39

ACTS OF THE END–TIME CHURCH

> *The Holy Spirit did not shut down in the Book of Acts chapter 28. The Day of Pentecost is already over 2,000 years long. We continue the Acts of the Apostles today. It went on to the Acts of the Early Church and now the Acts of the End-Time Church. The book of Acts described the day of small things, simply laying the foundation for us today.*

THE "DAYS OF PENTECOST" CONTINUE. SINCE PENTECOST, the Spirit of God, like a mighty wind, has been moving in a new and powerful way across the globe into all the dark places of the earth. The Early Church and the apostles did their part, recorded in the book of Acts, but that was not all the Holy Spirit did, has done or is doing. Now, we in this generation must add our part to the Acts of the Holy Spirit.

The wind of the Spirit is on the move, and we must move with it. No matter where you are or how dark it is, you must believe that the wind of the Spirit of God is blowing right there, and if you speak the Word, there will be light, salvations, deliverances, healings and miracles. So be bold, and speak the Word wherever you are. You will see results, because the wind of the Spirit is blowing and has already gone ahead of you.

FIRST SAMPLING

> *The early Christians are not our role models. Jesus is! The Book of Acts does not describe the climax of God's power, but a first sampling of the potential of the Holy Spirit. Trust God to infinity; He has no maximum!*

THE STORY OF THE COMING OF THE HOLY SPIRIT AND THE lives of the first apostles and the blossoming church are only a first sampling of the possibilities of Holy Spirit ministry. The field is open to us. Christ said, "Most assuredly, I say to you, he who believes in Me, the works that I do he will do also; and greater works than these he will do..." (John 14:12). Jesus is our example. Paul prayed "that the eyes of your understanding being enlightened; that you may know...what is the exceeding greatness of His power toward us who believe, according to the working of His mighty power which He worked in Christ when He raised Him from the dead and seated Him at His right hand in the heavenly places" (Ephesians 1:18-20).

TODAY

In this age, there are mass conversions in some of the toughest parts of the globe. Healings, miracles and signs abound in the Church. The truth of the Word of God is being experienced today, even as it was in the Early Church, and it is all by the power of the Holy Spirit.

SOMETHING POSITIVE IS HAPPENING TO PEOPLE TODAY. IT carries every Bible mark of what the Lord promised in Scripture: "'And it shall come to pass in the last days,' says God, 'that I will pour out of My Spirit on all flesh; your sons and your daughters shall prophesy, your young men shall see visions, your old men shall dream dreams. And on My menservants and on My maidservants I will pour out My Spirit in those days; and they shall prophesy'" (Acts 2:17, 18). God is keeping His word, and Jesus is baptizing in the Holy Spirit. There is no argument against it. It is happening, and it will happen to you.

CARRIED AWAY

> *The river of God is forceful! When our lives relate to His purposes, we are carried along as He sweeps from the eternal past to the eternal future. Allow yourself to be "carried away" by the Holy Spirit.*

BEFORE HE WAS APOSTLE PAUL, HE WAS SAUL. HE COLLECTED letters from the chief priests and religious leaders of his time to authorize him to persecute the Church. On the road to Damascus, the Lord appeared to Him. "Saul, Saul, why are you persecuting Me? It is hard for you to kick against the goads" (Acts 26:14). Saul was going against the currents of destiny. When he surrendered to Jesus, he entered the currents of the Holy Spirit and became a mighty apostle God would use to impact billions of believers. If the life you are leading is not worthwhile, try something new—a life authored by the Holy Spirit.

FIRE IN THE STOVE

> *No matter who you are or what your past is, you too can be used by God mightily. If you are fired up, He will use you. Just surrender to Him and let the Holy Spirit empower you for prayer, for study, for worship and for preaching to go to the nations, and you will see the signs and wonders that will follow (2 Timothy 2:20, 21).*

WHY DOES GOD USE SOME PEOPLE AND NOT OTHERS? Imagine you have two stoves at home. One is hot and one is cold, and you want to make yourself a cup of coffee. Which one of the two would you use? THE HOT ONE, of course. Do you get the point? That is the reason why God can use some and not others. Many people pray, "Use me Lord," but that is the wrong way round. Rather, pray, "Lord, make me useable." His fire makes us useable. The useable He uses automatically! Hallelujah.

FAITH LIKE A
MUSTARD SEED

"...For assuredly, I say to you, if you have faith
as a mustard seed, you will say to this mountain,
'Move from here to there,' and it will move;
and nothing will be impossible for you."

MATTHEW 17:20

WINGS OF FAITH

> *At the core of the fruit of the Spirit—love, kindness, gentleness, etc.—is the seed of unlimited power. The Christian is neither a timid nor tamed species. We may turn the other cheek and suffer persecution for His sake, but rest assured, we carry in our being the full dead-raising, hell-crushing, transforming power of the Holy Spirit. We have faith to move mountains and to raise valleys. With God nothing shall be impossible to us (Luke 1:37).*

NO TASK IS BIGGER THAN ANOTHER WHEN MEASURED BY faith. A fence, a house, a hill or a mountain makes no difference to a bird flying over them or to the person who soars on wings of faith. What God has called you to do is only possible through faith; as you walk (and fly) in faith, you will be able to live and move in the Holy Spirit in new ways.

SOARING – NOT SNORING

> *By faith, we "mount up on wings as eagles" (Isaiah 40:31). Soaring, not snoring! Don't snore through life, sleeping as you face life's obstacles. Soar over them as you spread your wings of faith today AND MOVE IN THE HOLY SPIRIT.*

WE LIVE BY FAITH AND NOT BY SIGHT (2 CORINTHIANS 5:7). Some situations in our lives may feel daunting because of the way they appear or feel to our physical senses. But wait! Don't buckle at the knees yet. Our faith is rooted in the Word of God. "I can do all things through Christ Who strengthens me" (Philippians 4:13).

BREAKING THROUGH THE CRUST OF UNBELIEF

> *You are meant to be an active volcano of Divine fire. You are not to be like a frosty snowcapped mountain—majestic but cold and powerless. Let the volcano blow off the top, and let the fire of the Holy Spirit flow from within (Hebrews 12:29).*

FAITH IS LIKE A VOLCANO, SEETHING AND SEEKING A WAY TO the brink. Once it breaks through unbelief's crust, a powerful eruption will follow. Whenever God can break through our crust of unbelief, a display of His awesome power occurs, defying all our moods and perplexities. How thick is the crust of our doubt? How resistant are we to trusting God? If we give up our unbelief, a secret channel will funnel God's fire to our relief—the fire of the Holy Spirit.

BELIEVERS, NOT BEGGARS

> *More than from love and generosity, God gives His Spirit to us out of necessity; God is desperate to fill us with His Spirit and empower us for His work. We do not need to beg or plead for this blessing. He is more than willing; He is ready. He is all-ready! Just believe and you shall receive.*

WHAT ABOUT "TARRYING IN JERUSALEM?" (LUKE 24:49). JESUS told the disciples to wait because, at that time, the Holy Spirit had not yet been given and would not be until Jesus was glorified (John 7:39). They had to wait for the historic moment—the Day of Pentecost. BUT NOW HE IS HERE. Pentecost is a fact, and you can experience it personally any day of the week. We have no pleading meetings, only receiving meetings. Jesus loves to fulfill His Word in our lives. We are believers, not beggars.

NOT BY MIGHT
OR FEELINGS

*"'...Not by might nor by power, but by
My Spirit,' says the Lord of hosts."*

ZECHARIAH 4:6

POWER AND FEELINGS

The baptism in the Spirit brings permanent power but not a permanent feeling of power. Fortunately, we don't measure power by feelings or by what we see. Spiritual power is latent strength in our spirit. But when circumstances call for it to be used, spiritual strength is there. The supply is immediate, matching the need as it arises. Don't let your dependence on feelings rob you of your spiritual victories.

WIRES, WHICH CAN CARRY 110,000 VOLTS, LOOK EXACTLY the same whether they are carrying current or not. Similarly, we cannot judge our own muscular power by FEELINGS but only by EXPERIMENT. Strong men don't feel their strength. They can't sit down and enjoy strength at the fireside. However, when asked to lift a heavy weight, they KNOW their strength and just do it. When we sit and rest, we don't feel full of power. We feel completely ordinary—we're not aware of His mighty power within us (2 Corinthians 10:1-6).

Nearly all prayers for power are really for a SENSE OF POWER—a desire to feel the throb or pulsation that accompanies power. That misses the point. Strength is evident when it is used. A man lifts dumbbells, and his strength shows. Some never do anything for God because they don't "feel" the power or strength. They keep on praying for what they probably already have. What a waste of time and effort! God's power will be there when it's needed. Rich men don't carry millions of dollars around with them. They draw on their resources whenever they please. We don't need to be trembling under the weight of Divine power from breakfast until dinner. We work because HE has all the power—not us. That's all that matters.

THE HOLY SPIRIT NEVER LEAVES

> *The Holy Spirit is fully present, whether we feel Him or not. His gifts and power do not depend on our ability to feel them. If we stand by faith on His Word, the Comforter will come and abide with you (John 14:16). We know He is always there, and He will never leave us nor forsake us, no matter the circumstances (Hebrews 13:5).*

I ONCE HEARD OF AN EVANGELIST WHO REFUSED TO ENTER the platform to preach. He said, "I cannot feel the anointing," and so instead of walking onto the platform, he cried and prayed backstage for God's presence. But he was wrong; the Holy Spirit is not a commodity but a person—the Third Person of the Trinity. Yet, no person can appear in percentages—a half or a quarter of themselves. The Holy Spirit is always fully present, even if we should be absent-minded or cannot feel Him. Sometimes, when preaching in front of hundreds of thousands of people, I do not feel His presence. What do I do? I remember that Jesus told us that the Holy Spirit will abide with us forever. I then appropriate that promise by faith. I preach the Word of God, which is always honored and confirmed by the Spirit of God. We do not always feel the power, but He is always there. The Holy Spirit never leaves us.

IT'S TIME TO PARTNER WITH THE HOLY SPIRIT

> *All non-God-inspired operations are temporary, but the Jesus-Holy Spirit partnership will last far beyond anything else that moves. This is part of God's order at creation and goes on forever—with or without us. We are free to be failures if we want—or heroes of faith.*

WHATEVER GOD DOES SHALL BE FOREVER. (ECCLESIASTES 3:14). This is as true about God's creation as it is true of our lives and ministry. We can choose to factor God into every aspect of our lives and be Christ-centered in our dealings, or we can choose to ignore the reality of God all together. But I personally want to challenge you to do more than put God into the equation; I want you to partner with God to solve the equation. Let Him help you with your destiny, your health, your family, your ministry, etc. Whatever concerns you, He is willing and able to be a part of the solution.

SUPERNATURAL WORKING POWER

"For it is God Who works in you both to will and to do for His good pleasure."

PHILIPPIANS 2:13

HOOKING THE LOAD TO THE LIFTING MACHINERY

> *If a 1,000 ton block of iron had to be lifted by crane, how much could you help? Suppose you could get a grip on it and tried to heave and pull? What difference would you make? There would be no difference, and it wouldn't help.*

WHAT ABOUT LIFTING THE WHOLE WORLD? THAT IS A TASK for God, through the power of His atoning death and resurrection. Do you think you take the load off His shoulders and do a kind of Hercules exchange? Is God almighty, and then He needs a little bit of extra help from us? Jesus said He had ALL power. That's surely enough! You may just as well leave it to the power of God. "Cast your burden on the Lord" (Psalm 55:22).

Does that mean that we should sit idle? By no means! Far from it, for you have a privileged and important part to play. What is it? What do hoist-operators do? They don't attempt to lift heavy weights with their own hands, but neither do they hang around with their hands in their pockets. They know what to do, and without them the load will never be lifted. They hook the load to the lifting machinery! That's what our job is. Don't try to lift everybody's burden all by yourself. That is what only God can do. Our simple task is to bring people to Him. The Gospel is the power of God to lift the entire world (Romans 1:16). There is power—plenty of power. Jesus said so (Matthew 28:18 KJV).

NO POWER NEEDED FOR DOING NOTHING

> *The vision of blood-washed world-continents can only be realized when we believe God and act on it. Do nothing and nothing happens. God doesn't need to give us inspiring visions to do what we can do, but rather what we cannot. We excel at being ordinary. Jesus chose us for the honor of the extraordinary. Catch the vision! People say 'I am not the visionary type.' But Joseph, who was a "dreamer," did not dream about the Promised Land. He rather appropriated for himself the Word of God to Abraham, Isaac and Jacob and "gave instructions concerning his bones" that his mummy should be carried with them when Israel entered Canaan (Hebrews 11:22).*

SOME PEOPLE PRAY FOR POWER, BUT DO NOTHING. WELL, nobody needs power for doing nothing. Open your spirit to the Spirit of God, and vision and power will flow like a mighty river. Jesus does not sit with sitters, nor sleep with sleepers, but He works with workers and endues them with the power of the Holy Spirit. He puts fight into timid rabbits and transforms pygmies into giants working alongside omniscience. Jesus changes our nesting habits, fills us with His Holy Spirit and makes the impossible possible.

THE WORLD IS WAITING

"And He (Jesus) said to them, 'Go into all the
world and preach the Gospel to every creature.
He who believes and is baptized will be saved;
but he who does not believe will be condemned.
And these signs will follow those who believe:
in My name they will cast out demons; they
will speak with new tongues; they will take up
serpents; and if they drink anything deadly,
it will by no means hurt them; they will lay
hands on the sick, and they will recover.'"

MARK 16:15-18

THE BATHTUB IS NOT BIG ENOUGH

> *We have to relearn, not to just how to preach the Gospel in churches, but also rediscover the highways and the byways where the lost are. The Supreme Commission of Jesus is for our own time.*

IF YOU WANT TO WIN SOULS, DON'T THROW YOUR NET INTO A bathtub. There are no fish there. At best, you will catch a piece of soap. If you have a heart for souls to be saved, throw your net into a river, the ocean or a lake. You have to go where the fish are, and that is wherever God sends you. If you wonder where the lake is, simply leave the sanctuary, step out of the church and onto the streets. That is where the harvest begins. As people flow past, they all need Jesus. We have become too comfortable behind our stained-glass windows; we urgently need to recover the highways and byways.

THE TIDE COMES IN

> *The Holy Spirit comes in like a mighty rushing wind, and when the Gospel is preached, it is with tidings of great joy (Luke 2:10). This Gospel is like the tide—as it rises, it moves everything in its way. It unlocks stuck callings and floats them in currents of greatness.*

I GREW UP AT THE MOUTH OF THE RIVER ELBE IN GERMANY. When the tide was out, we boys played around the barges stuck in the mud. In my mind, they were impossible to shift or move. But then the tide came in. Suddenly, the barges floated. I could move them from the pier with one foot. When we preach the Gospel, the tide comes in, the immovable become movable, the incurable curable and the impossible possible. Let's trust God!

BOTTOMLESS HOPE

> *When the tide comes in, it doesn't just lift one or two ships, but every boat—except those that have no bottom. But there is hope for even those ships; they can be repaired by the Holy Spirit. Renewed and restored, those ships rise to new service and ministry.*

THE POWER OF THE HOLY SPIRIT IS ABLE TO TRANSCEND individual needs and moves into families, communities and cities. Don't limit the effect and power of the Holy Spirit. The Holy Spirit agenda is always greater than one person, one family or even one community. When the Holy Spirit moves, more than one life is touched. When Peter went to Cornelius' house to minister, the Holy Spirit fell not just on him but the entire household (Acts 10). When Philip ministered to the Ethiopian eunuch, a whole nation was impacted (Acts 8:26-40).

CHOOSE FAITH!

"But Joshua the son of Nun and Caleb the son of Jephunneh, who were among those who had spied out the land, tore their clothes; and they spoke to all the congregation of the children of Israel, saying: 'The land we passed through to spy out is an exceedingly good land. If the Lord delights in us, then He will bring us into this land and give it to us, 'a land which flows with milk and honey.' Only do not rebel against the Lord, nor fear the people of the land, for they are our bread; their protection has departed from them, and the Lord is with us. Do not fear them.'"

NUMBERS 14:6-9

EMPTY GRAVE OR UPPER ROOM

Moses said, "I have set before you life and death, blessing and cursing; therefore choose life" (Deuteronomy 30:19). You have the choice to focus on the questions that lead to doubt, discouragement and death or the answers that lead to life, hope and blessings. The Holy Spirit gives you the answers and power for fulfilled living.

AFTER JESUS HAD RISEN GLORIOUSLY FROM THE DEAD, JOHN and Peter were the first to step into His grave. They might have sat for a long time and like scholars examined the DNA of the shroud. If they had continued there, they might have written scientific books for posterity. But thank God, they left the grave, found the Upper Room, and there the fire fell.

SEEKING TO HONOR MAN OR GOD?

Let's not be man-pleasers but God-pleasers. He who is immune to the praise of man is also immune to the criticism of man. Let the Lord be your glory and the lifter of your head.

FEAR PLAYS INTO THE HANDS OF THE DEVIL. HE CAN DO NO real damage except to make us fear that he can. The devil is a con artist. Balaam was forced to speak the truth (Numbers 22-24). He wound up showing us that God's people are not for cursing. We are immune. We are redeemed. What was true of God's redeemed people then is true of the redeemed today. Fear hears the shout of Goliath, but faith hears the shout of the King of kings.

IMMUNITY

> *Against all attacks of the devil, the Christian carries the shield of faith. It is bulletproof. We enjoy immunity from devil control and enjoy salvation, victory and freedom. We can be bold, impregnable through faith in the redemptive blood of Christ and the Holy Spirit.*

A NEWS CHANNEL ONCE CRITICIZED ME AND MY WORK. Ministers called me and said, "Reinhard, you must defend yourself." I fell on my knees and said, "Lord what shall I do?" The Holy Spirit spoke to me, "You are manning a combine-harvester on My harvest-field. Do not stop it just to catch a mouse!" Instead of defending myself, I always speak about my next Gospel crusade. That makes me happy and the devil mad. The Lord is the One Who vindicates me. On that day, I want to hear, "Well done, good and faithful servant" (Matthew 25:21).

REFLECT HIS GLORY

> *God's glory was reflected in the jewels in the High Priest's breastplate (Exodus 28:15-21). Splashes of prismatic color would cross the curtain walls reflecting only the glory of the Lord. It is a perfect picture. We have no glory of our own, however gem-like our shining personal talents. The only true light comes from Jesus Christ. We are witnesses to that light (John 1:8) as we turn our faces to Him and reflect what Jesus was and is. Unless we catch that light in our own lives, nobody will see it. The gifts of the Spirit are His gifts, not our natural talents or graces.*

WHATEVER WE CAN DO, WHATEVER WE CAN BE, WHATEVER we should do, whether by natural or supernatural abilities, the Spirit of God must burn and shine through it all that there may be glory in the Church by Christ Jesus. "For Yours is the Kingdom and the power and the glory forever. Amen" (Matthew 6:13).

IT'S GO TIME

"Then Philip went down to the city of Samaria and preached Christ to them. And the multitudes with one accord heeded the things spoken by Philip, hearing and seeing the miracles which he did. For unclean spirits, crying with a loud voice, came out of many who were possessed; and many who were paralyzed and lame were healed. And there was great joy in that city."

ACTS 8:5-8

THIS IS NO SIMULATOR

Having read this book, you have reached the "rocket of God." All engines and systems are hot and ready for takeoff. But there is only one missing element: You. Come on! Step into the cockpit, and let the Holy Spirit shoot you into the orbit of God's supreme purposes.

ASTRONAUTS LOG HUNDREDS OF HOURS ON SIMULATORS practicing technical and life skills critical to their mission success. But a simulator is just that—a simulation, not the real thing. In the end, astronauts must step out from their comfort and safety zones and get onto the launch pad for the mission. In the same way, the Holy Spirit waits to launch you into your destiny. It is time to step into the nose of the rocket with the Holy Spirit, and into the life of wonder—full of miracles and possibilities.

HOLY SPIRIT
CHRONICLES

SECTION 9:

ENTERING A LIFE OF FIRE–
HOW TO RECEIVE THE
BAPTISM IN THE HOLY SPIRIT

"And it happened, while Apollos was at Corinth, that Paul, having passed through the upper regions, came to Ephesus. And finding some disciples he said to them, 'Did you receive the Holy Spirit when you believed?' So they said to him, 'We have not so much as heard whether there is a Holy Spirit.' And he said to them, 'Into what then were you baptized?' So they said, 'Into John's baptism.' Then Paul said, 'John indeed baptized with a baptism of repentance, saying to the people that they should believe on Him who would come after him, that is, on Christ Jesus.' When they heard this, they were baptized in the name of the Lord Jesus. And when Paul had laid hands on them, the Holy Spirit came upon them, and they spoke with tongues and prophesied."

ACTS 19:1-6

PART ONE:
THE BAPTISM IN THE HOLY
SPIRIT – WHAT IT IS

The baptism in the Holy Spirit is so important to the life and ministry of the believer. In order to give you a sound biblical understanding of the baptism of the Holy Spirit, I have put together the sequence of events that mark the timeline leading up to Pentecost and beyond. These are Holy Spirit Chronicles.

THE EDICT

The most wonderful sound ever heard was about to fall on the ears of the tens of thousands of people gathered in the Temple courts at Jerusalem. The final rituals of a national festival were taking place. All eyes followed a golden vessel filled with water and wine. A drink offering was ready to be poured out to the Lord.

A priest lifted the gleaming vessel in the sunshine and paused. Silence fell as the people strained to hear the sacred water splashing into a bronze bowl at the altar. Then came the interruption: a voice not known for 1,000 years. A voice that made the spine tingle. It was the voice of Jesus Christ, the Son of God. He was the Word Who had spoken in the beginning and called forth heaven and earth into existence. Now, at Jerusalem, He stood and issued a royal and Divine edict, changing the dispensation of God:

> "If anyone thirsts, let him come to Me and drink. He who believes in Me, as the Scripture has said, out of his heart will flow rivers of living water" (John 7:37, 38).

STREAMS IN THE DESERT

"Rivers of living water!" Not bottles, but rivers, fresh, lively, sparkling, abundant and unending. Some people live for what comes out of a bottle. The world's supermarkets have very little that is fresh. Prepackaged pleasure is big business, with canned music, films and books. Television provides the highlights of life for millions of people as they watch others live or pretending to live. This even includes children, who forget how to play.

LIVE NOW!

People are always "going to" live...after things change, after working hours, when they have money, when they get married, retire or go on holiday. Jesus came to give us life NOW. NO WAITING but wherever we are and whatever we are doing. He makes life live.

HISTORICAL BLACKBOARD

God wrote His plan for Israel while they were in the wilderness across a blackboard 40 years wide. The Israelites did not have to drink stale, flat water from skins. The Lord opened bubbling streams from a rock (Exodus 17:1-7). The Temple drink offering was a celebration in memory of that wilderness water (Numbers 20:1-13). Jesus, however, gave it a new and glorious meaning – a symbol of the outpouring of the Holy Spirit.

ONLY JESUS

THIS JESUS! Nobody else had ever dared to make such an amazing claim and to then fulfill it. He would ascend to glory, where Creation began, and change the order of things. Something not known before would surge from heaven to earth. He called it "the promise of the Father" (Acts 1:4 KJV). THE promise. Out of over 8,000 promises in God's Word, the designation of THE promise makes it stand out singularly and significantly alone. Christ made it His own promise. The Father's gift to Him is His gift to us, as John the Baptist said:

"I did not know Him, but He who sent me to baptize with water said to me, 'Upon Whom you see the Spirit descending, and remaining on Him, this is He who baptizes with the Holy Spirit.' And I have seen and testified that this is the Son of God" (John 1:33, 34).

WHEN WORDS FAIL

John used a different expression here instead of "rivers of living water." Scripture has many other terms such as: Being baptized in holy fire (Matthew 3:11; Luke 3:16); "endued with power" (Luke 24:49); anointed with the oil of God; immersed in the Spirit; "filled with the Spirit" (Ephesians 5:18 NIV); walking, praying or living in the Spirit (Galatians 5:25; Romans 8:26); our bodies being temples of the Holy Spirit (1 Corinthians 6:19); having "another Comforter" besides Christ Himself (John 14:16 KJV).

PICTURE GALLERY

These are sketches, but color and details have to be added. The Bible is a picture gallery of the Holy Spirit in operation; it portrays signs, wonders and miracles. It shows men looking as if "they had been with Jesus," the world turned upside down, and people coming to "know the Lord" and enjoying a new experience. These were not just religious enthusiasts or church-goers, but a new breed with vibrant faith. Paul says that God "...made us alive with Christ even when we were dead in transgressions..." (Ephesians 2:5 NIV) and that we are "...strengthened with all power according to His glorious might" (Colossians 1:11 NIV). The Lord Jesus Christ Himself promised it:

> "'But you shall receive power when the Holy Spirit comes upon you'" (Acts 1:8).

We, as born again believers, are special; we are saints, and the baptism in the Spirit is Christ's next major experience for us. Jesus alone made it possible when He died, rose and sat down at the right hand of the Majesty on High. What a gift!

WHO IS THE HOLY SPIRIT?

The Lord does not send publicity by heavenly mail to tell us who He is. The works performed by His Spirit are seen on earth. The Holy Spirit is a Person; He is God in action. Creation came as "the Spirit of God was hovering over the face of the waters" (Genesis 1:2). Then, when God chose His servants, the power of the Holy Spirit rested upon them:

> "Then Moses said to the Israelites, 'See, the Lord has chosen Bezalel son of Uri, the son of Hur, of the tribe of Judah, and He has filled him with the Spirit of God, with wisdom, with understanding, with knowledge and with all kinds of skills...And He has given both him and Oholiab son of Ahisamak, of the tribe of Dan, the ability to teach others'" (Exodus 35:30, 31, 34 NIV).

> "The Spirit of the Lord came upon him [Othniel], and he judged Israel" (Judges 3:10).

> The Spirit "clothed Gideon with Himself" (Judges 6:34 AMP), and Gideon defended Israel (Judges 6:11–8:35). The Spirit moved Samson to acts of supernatural strength (Judges 13:1–16:31). The Spirit of the Lord came upon Jephtha and delivered Israel's foes into his hands (Judges 11:1–12:7).

> After these judges, the prophet Samuel guided an entire nation for a lifetime. How? "Holy men of God spoke {as they were} moved by the Holy Spirit" (2 Peter 1:21). The prophet Micah testified, "I am full of power by the Spirit of the Lord" (Micah 3:8 KJV).

These are portraits of the Holy Spirit. This is that Spirit whom Christ promised: the Spirit of wisdom and knowledge, creative, empowering, healing, the Spirit of strength, confidence, and virtue.

God's power is not a kind of supercharge for people already gifted with great personality and drive, but is for those who need it–the weak and the unknown. "He gives power to the weak, and to those who have no might He increases strength" (Isaiah 40:29).

FOUR GREAT PICTURES

Four of the pictures in the Bible gallery should be examined carefully.

THE PROPHET'S WISH

The first picture: Moses put his hands on 70 elders at the Tent of Meeting, and the Spirit of God came upon them. At that moment back in the camp, Eldad and Medad were also endued and began to prophesy. A young man ran to tell Moses. Joshua thought Moses should have a monopoly on prophesying and urged, "Moses, my lord, stop them!" Far from objecting, Moses said, "Are you jealous for my sake? I wish that all the Lord's people were prophets and that the Lord would put His Spirit on them!" (Numbers 11:24-29 NIV).

Seventy at once! That was the most for over 1,200 years. The experience was rare, usually temporary and only for individuals. However, Moses' wish lay in many hearts while long centuries passed.

BRIGHT SKIES

The second picture: The Temple Solomon had built was in full operation, but sin had weakened the nation. A prophet stood in Jerusalem, bringing a warning of judgment. Through the telescope of prophecy, Joel had seen distant skies black with war clouds, terror and destruction, with Israel laid waste which, as we now know, proved Joel a true prophet. However, Joel was telling Israel more. Beyond the gathering storm, he saw bright skies, not merely recovery, but a wonderful New Thing.

"And afterward, I will pour out My Spirit upon all people. Your sons and daughters will prophesy, your old men will dream dreams, your young men will see visions. Even on My servants, both men and women, I will pour out My Spirit in those days. I will show wonders in the heavens and on the earth, blood and fire and billows of smoke'" (Joel 2:28-30 NIV).

ALL PRIVILEGED

In those days, young slave girls poured water on the hands of their mistresses to wash them, but God promised to pour out His Spirit even on those servants. In fact, this prophecy meant that the HOLY SPIRIT WOULD BE POURED OUT WORLDWIDE UPON ALL MANNER OF PEOPLE regardless of their station in life.

This was sensational. What He had once granted to only a handful of His chosen servants would be a privilege everyone could call his own. It was too hard for many to imagine or believe. But God said it, and His Word stands forever.

A PROPHET IN LEATHER GARMENTS

The third picture: John the Baptist, in leather clothing, stood on the bank of the Jordan River. He was the first prophet of God in 400 years. Crowds came out to hear him and be baptized. His thunderous message called on Israel to repent and prepare because the long awaited Coming One would appear.

> "I baptize you with water for repentance. But after me will come One who is more powerful than I, Whose sandals I am not fit to carry. He will baptize you with the Holy Spirit and with fire" (Matthew 3:11 NIV).

NO ORDINARY BAPTIST

Twenty-four hours later, among the candidates for baptism, John saw a young man wading through the waters and stood aghast: "YOU! JESUS! I am not worthy to baptize You. You should baptize me!" God had shown John that Jesus was that promised "One who was to come" (Matthew 11:3; Luke 7:19, 20 NIV). He would perform a rite far greater than John in the Jordan. Jesus the Baptist would not use a physical element, water, but heavenly fire, which is a spiritual element. John stood in the cold waters of the Jordan, but Jesus stood in a river of liquid fire. John had baptized for a few short days; Jesus would baptize down through the ages—not just one group on the Day of Pentecost, but "all flesh." He is doing so even now, some 700,000 days later!

PROMISE KEEPERS

The fourth picture: Fearing the authorities who had executed Jesus, 120 disciples came together quietly. Jesus had said, "Stay in the city [Jerusalem] until you have been clothed with power from on high" (Luke 24:49 NIV). They sat and waited, and the world forgot them. Nothing happened; no marvels occurred. Everything seemed so ordinary.

DAYS OF PENTECOST

The tenth day was a Sunday, the Feast of Weeks, also called Pentecost. At nine in the morning, a Temple priest lifted the bread of the first fruits and waved it before the Lord. As if this were a signal for the ascended Christ, a divine tornado tore through the skies above Jerusalem.

Jesus Himself had broken through the heavens in His shattering and victorious Ascension. Now through the opened skies there was a Descension. The Holy Spirit came, demonstrating that the way into the heavens was open. Praise God, it has never been closed since! When the curtain of the Temple was ripped as Jesus died, the priests probably tried to stitch it together again. Nobody can stitch up this rent in the heavens—not even the devil and all his minions. It is a new and living way, open forever.

AMBER FLAMES

Moses saw God as fire in the bush. Now through this door of glory, which no man could shut, the same fire, the Holy Spirit, came. Amber flames settled in burning beauty upon the head of each waiting disciple. Glory that filled all heaven now crowded into the breasts of those present. The Holy Spirit was in them and on them. Men had never experienced it before. There were no words to describe it. This was unutterable. Then God gave them words, new tongues and languages to tell "the wonderful works of God" (Acts 2:11 KJV) like inspired psalmists.

COMFORTED

The explanation is simple: The disciples belonged to Christ. He said so, and as long as He was with them on earth, they could do marvelous works. Then He ascended to God, and they felt lonely and frightened. However, the Lord had made a promise: He would send another Helper, the Holy Spirit (John 14:16).

The word "comforter" (*paraclete*) implies "someone walking by your side." For three and a half years, Jesus was with them day and night, teaching them and giving them hope for this life and eternity. These peasants had comforting news from the Master–Christ Himself. But in His absence physically on earth, they would need another person to step in that role of Comforter–the Third Person of the Trinity, The Holy Spirit.

THE HELPER IS HERE!

The word "Helper" suggests someone readily available to give assistance when necessary. Jesus had been by their sides for over three years, and He was their first great Helper, Companion and Comforter. Then that other Person, another Helper, the Holy Spirit, came on the Day of Pentecost. It was like having Jesus with them again, and they could carry out the Great Commission to preach the Gospel, heal the sick, cast out devils and work wonders as before–in short, the work of witnessing, which is the privilege and responsibility of every born-again person (Matthew 28:19, 20; Mark 16:15-18).

JOINT HEIRS

The same situation exists for us. We are joint heirs of the same promise. First, we must come to Christ and give ourselves to Him, and then we can receive the power baptism. Our very lives should be evidence of His Resurrection. It is more than talk that is needed–it is people manifesting the fullness of the Spirit.

DIPPED IN FIRE

The word "baptism" did not have a religious meaning originally. It is from the trade of dyeing fabrics. The English equivalent is 'dipping.' The cloth or garment is dipped into the dye, and the cloth takes on the color or character of the dye. When Christ baptizes us in the Spirit, we partake of the "color" or character of the Spirit, partakers of the divine nature (2 Peter 1:4). The Spirit is in us, and we are in the Spirit. We are people of the Holy Spirit. Dipped in Fire!

THE BAPTISM AND OTHER WORKINGS

SALVATION AND MORE

We receive salvation and are born again through the Holy Spirit. But that is not the end of His work. His activities are manifold. He empowers us for witnessing. The baptism in the Spirit means that people saved by grace and born again can have new experiences and become Spirit-energized witnesses for Christ.

NOT AN OPTION

How necessary is the baptism of the Holy Spirit? It was vital even for the disciples who had healed the sick and cast out demons. That was possible only as long as Christ was by their sides. The Lord Jesus told them to wait until they were endued with the Spirit before they went forth into the fields for service. Mary, the mother of Christ, was one example. She had certainly known the Holy Spirit in her life to bring about the birth of Jesus, but she too waited at Jerusalem for this further work of the Spirit, called "the promise of the Father." If she needed it, we all do (Acts 1:4 KJV).

ENDUED WITH POWER

It was not just seeing Jesus or hearing His voice which made the disciples the great people they were, because "some believed and some doubted"

(Matthew 28:17; Mark 16:13, 14; Luke 24:41), but it happened through the Holy Spirit baptism. They shut the door when they met for fear of the Jews (John 20:19). They certainly did not shout in the streets, "Jesus is alive!" They met secretly, at first away in Galilee, and they even went fishing (John 21). All that changed, however, on the Day of Pentecost. Instead of their being afraid of the Jewish crowds, the crowds trembled before them and cried out, "Brothers, what shall we do?" (Acts 2:37 NIV). This was as Jesus said:

"But you will receive power when the Holy Spirit comes on you; and you will be My witnesses...to the ends of the earth'" (Acts 1:8 NIV).

HOW IT FIRST HAPPENED

A SOUND FROM HEAVEN

Now we look again at the fourth picture:

"When the Day of Pentecost had fully come, they were all with one accord in one place. And suddenly there came a sound from heaven, as of a rushing mighty wind, and it filled the whole house where they were sitting. Then there appeared to them divided tongues, as of fire, and one sat upon each of them. And they were all filled with the Holy Spirit and began to speak with other tongues, as the Spirit gave them utterance" (Acts 2:1-4).

NO EMPTY PROMISES

What Divine power and glory! This second chapter of Acts is noisy and action-packed. The heavenly Father does not make empty promises, just to build up our hopes and then laugh at us. Christ had said, "Go into all the world..." (Mark 16:15 NIV). The moment those "tongues of fire" touched their heads it put the "go" into them. God acted, and then they acted. Divine action caused human reaction, which is why this book is called the Acts of the Apostles.

THE OUTFLOW

There was an inflow from heaven, and there had to be an outflow. "Out of his heart shall flow rivers" (John 7:38), not just "into." It was not for emotional satisfaction. The disciples did not say, "Let us have a prayer meeting for power like this every week." They never again asked for power for themselves, because they knew that they had it already. The apostle Peter said to the cripple at the Gate Beautiful, "What I do have I give to you" (Acts 3:6 NIV).

FIRE GOSPEL

Nor did they just sit, appointing a chairman and passing resolutions on social problems. They could not contain themselves! They had to be up and doing. Peter stood, electrified. And the Christian age began; the world heard the first Gospel sermon. Of course, it was a Fire Gospel.

FRUITFUL EVANGELISM

The result? Three thousand people received salvation. That was the reason for Pentecost. In fact, the Trinity, the whole Godhead, set the plans of salvation and evangelism into motion. The Father joined with the ascended Lord to send the Spirit to save a lost world (Isaiah 48:16). That is the main purpose of the baptism in the Spirit. That is what God is doing: saving people. What are we doing? This baptism is not for thrills, but to help us work alongside the Lord. We know why Jesus and the Holy Spirit came. Why are WE here?

THE HOLY SPIRIT DIFFERENCE

What a day Pentecost was! "Rivers" flowed that eventually flooded the Roman Empire. People sigh and wish they were back in the days of the Early Church, but it was neither the days nor the men which made the times special. It was the baptism in the Holy Spirit. Without it, the disciples would probably have gone back to being fishermen in Galilee and grown old telling tales of strange events when they were young. Instead, they changed the world. That baptism is for all today.

FOR TODAY

Some people want to deprive believers today, saying the baptism in the Spirit with signs following was only for the first believers "until the Church got under way;" they suggest that we have to manage without the miraculous gifts of those believers. That would make the Early Christians an elite group, as if we could not be Christians in the way they were. However, not a word in the Bible suggests such a thing. It is a theory invented by unbelief. In fact, when Paul went to Ephesus 20 years after the Church had been well planted, 12 people were baptized in the Spirit (Acts 19:6, 7).

PENTECOST FOR ALL GENERATIONS

Every generation needs Pentecost. In A.D. 30, the world population was one hundred million. Today it is over seven billion and growing rapidly. Ten times more people today than in the first century do not know about Jesus. The Church still needs planting. Unbelief and complete ignorance of God exist everywhere. Surely our need for the power of the Holy Spirit is far more desperate.

Therefore, I want to explain to you carefully, from the Bible itself, why and how that same baptism is for us today. Read what Peter preached to the multitude on the Day of Pentecost, under the anointing of the Spirit, when he explained who could be baptized in the Holy Spirit:

> "For the promise is to you and to your children, and to all who are afar off, as many as the Lord our God will call" (Acts 2:39).

TO YOU

First, Peter said it is "to you," the very people he had just accused saying, "Ye have taken [Jesus], and by wicked hands have crucified and slain [Him]" (Acts 2:23 KJV). Yet he announced, "Repent, and be baptized every one of you in the name of Jesus Christ for the forgiveness of your sins. And you will receive the gift of the Holy Spirit" (Acts 2:38 NIV). These were the same people that Jesus had called "an evil generation" (Luke 11:29), "faithless and perverse" (Matthew 17:17; Luke 9:41).

TO YOUR CHILDREN

Second, he said it is "to your children," the next generation. Some people would not become parents until later. It could be that 100 years after the Day of Pentecost, people would receive this blessing and speak in tongues. One woman mentioned in Luke 2:36 had been a widow for 84 years. However, the word "children" referred not only to their families, but also to their descendants, that is, the children of Israel.

TO ALL THAT ARE FAR OFF

Third, Peter said, "to all that are far off," that is, in time and distance, at the ends of the earth where Christ had commissioned the Church to take the Gospel (Matthew 28:19, 20; Mark 16:15, 16). This would take many years, far beyond the apostolic age. New Zealand, for example, would be one of the ends of the earth; no missionary arrived there until 1814. Indeed, the task is not completed even today; therefore, we still need that same power.

TO EVERYONE WHOM THE LORD OUR GOD CALLS

Fourth, Peter hammered it home, "every one whom the Lord our God calls to Him." Those "God calls" are those who come to Christ. "No one can come to Me unless the Father who sent Me draws Him"

(John 6:44 NIV). All believers are called and are promised the same gift of the Holy Spirit that Peter and his 119 friends had just received. Do what the disciples did, and you will get what the disciples got. Believe God's promises are given to us all, "And be not drunk with wine…but be filled with the Spirit" (Ephesians 5:18 KJV).

DIRECT FROM JESUS

Only Jesus is the Baptizer, nobody else. Do not settle for a secondhand experience. Have your own Pentecost. Do not try to cash in on someone else's experience in a charismatic meeting. The fire of the Holy Spirit did not arrive in one big, general flame so that all could gather and warm themselves, conducting cozy conferences. Rather, it came in separate "tongues," little flames that "sat upon each of them" (Acts 2:3). This was very significant. Those tongues of fire were in fact potent and portable power stations which would move with the people wherever they went.

AGLOW WITH THE SPIRIT

We live in a spiritually dark and cold world. The best way not to freeze is to be aglow with the Holy Spirit. God will light a fire on the altar of your own heart so that you can be a fire-starter. Warm others; do not depend on others to warm you!

PART TWO: THE BAPTISM IN THE HOLY SPIRIT – HOW TO RECEIVE IT

You would think that such a precious gift as the Holy Spirit would be complicated to receive. But on the contrary, it is quite simple. Right where you are now you can receive the baptism in the Holy Spirit. In this session, I give you some very simple teachings on how to receive the Holy Spirit.

BELIEVING THE GIVER

Thousands of people come into our campaign meetings as unbelievers. Some of them are really far away from God: wicked, immoral, addicted, bound by the occult or working hard for religions that do nothing for them. They must first receive salvation. Paul said to converts in his day, "You were washed clean" (1 Corinthians 6:11 AMP). Perhaps unclean spirits had previously occupied their bodies. Yet we see hundreds of thousands of such people become temples of the Holy Spirit. How? There are only two conditions: one, repentance, and two, faith in the Lord Jesus Christ.

> "Then Peter said to them, 'Repent, and let every one of you be baptized in the name of Jesus Christ for the remission of sins; and you shall receive the gift of the Holy Spirit'" (Acts 2:38).

REPENTANCE

Jesus said: "I will ask the Father, and He will give you another Helper...The world cannot accept Him'" (John 14:16, 17 NIV). Peter said: "Repent ye therefore, and be converted, that your sins may be blotted out, when times of refreshing shall come from the presence of the Lord. Repent…for the remission of sins, and ye shall receive the gift of the Holy Spirit" (Acts 3:19; 2:38 KJV).

A HOLY GIFT

The Holy Spirit is a holy Being. The Bible uses the image of a dove for the Holy Spirit. A dove is a clean bird; it will not build its nest on a dunghill. The Holy Spirit will not settle in a sinful life; He is too sensitive. Heavenly waters do not flow through polluted channels—through neither foul minds nor foul mouths.

BLOOD WASHED

The Holy Spirit is only for the blood-washed sons and daughters of God. Nobody can be good enough until cleansed in Calvary's fountain. Blood comes before fire. No other cleansing is necessary or possible. We cannot make ourselves more holy or more worthy than the blood of Jesus already makes us. The Holy Spirit is a gift and cannot be earned.

FAITH

"And without faith it is impossible to please God, because anyone who comes to Him must believe that He exists and that He rewards those who earnestly seek Him" (Hebrews 11:6 NIV).

"By this He meant the Spirit, Whom those who believed in Him were later to receive" (John 7:39 NIV).

"You foolish Galatians! Did you receive the Spirit by observing the law, or by believing what you heard?" (Galatians 3:1, 2 NIV).

COME WITH BOLDNESS

To come to Jesus begging and pleading is not having faith at all. FAITH INVOLVES TAKING. You do not need to persuade Jesus Christ to be kind and baptize you in His holy fire. He has already promised. Come with boldness to collect what He is offering you. It is a gift, and you must believe the Giver before you reach out to receive what the Giver is giving.

NO MORE TARRYING

What about "waiting in Jerusalem?" Jesus told the disciples to wait, but then the Holy Spirit "had not been given, since Jesus had not yet been glorified" (John 7:39 NIV). They had to wait for the historic moment. BUT NOW HE IS HERE. Pentecost is a fact, and you can experience it personally. We have no pleading meetings, only receiving meetings. Jesus loves to fulfill His Word in our lives. We are believers, not beggars.

THE HOLY LANGUAGE

When we receive the original baptism in the Spirit, the original signs will follow.

> "All of them were filled with the Holy Spirit and began to speak in other tongues as the Spirit enabled them" (Acts 2:4 NIV).

How? The 120 disciples were praising the Lord. Then came "a rushing mighty wind" (Acts 2:2) and the tongues of flame, and their hearts exploded with joy. They opened their mouths to speak, and the Spirit gave them utterance in languages unknown to them. Just like that.

SAME EFFECT

If we receive the same baptism, it must have the same effect. Jesus the Baptizer has not changed, nor have His methods. In God's kingdom, we are not copies of copies, but originals from The Original, JESUS CHRIST. When we experience the baptism in the Holy Spirit, we do not receive leftovers but the original experience.

TONGUES

The ability to speak in tongues is mentioned throughout the book of Acts:

> "The circumcised believers who had come with Peter were astonished that the gift of the Holy Spirit had been poured out even on the Gentiles. For they heard them speaking in tongues and praising God" (Acts 10:45, 46 NIV).

Speaking in tongues was taken by the apostle as evidence of the baptism in the Holy Spirit. Simon the Sorcerer "saw" this supernatural manifestation of the Spirit (Acts 8:17-19). Paul received the baptism (Acts 9:17) and said he spoke with tongues (1 Corinthians 14:18). On other occasions, the same thing is reported: Acts 11:17; 13:52; 19:6.

On the Day of Pentecost, Peter explained what was happening by quoting Joel (Acts 2:17-19). Joel had prophesied that people would prophesy. When they spoke with tongues, Peter said, "This is that" (Acts 2:16 KJV). Speaking with tongues, when interpreted, is prophecy.

A TANGIBLE SIGN

What better sign could God give to make us confident that the Holy Spirit is within and upon us as we go out to preach the Gospel? When we feel weak and fearful and hard pressed as Paul did (1 Corinthians 2:3), the wonder of tongues assures us. Without some outward manifestation, we could pray forever without being sure, and that is exactly what has happened.

THE HOLY SPIRIT'S SECRET CODE

What a wonderful thing! Paul described speaking in tongues as telling secrets to God (1 Corinthians 14:2). Tongues is the only language the devil cannot understand. The arch-confuser is totally confused himself, because he does not even know the alphabet of the Holy Spirit. Satan cannot crack the Holy Spirit's secret code, which puts us in touch with the throne of heaven.

BUILT FOR PRAYER

Our bodies are "temples of the Holy Spirit" (1 Corinthians 6:19 NIV). Jesus said a temple was a house of prayer (Matthew 21:13; Mark 11:17). If our bodies are temples, houses of prayer in which the Spirit dwells, then He will pray through us pure and powerful prayers reaching the throne of God. The Spirit loves to pray, and that is why the Spirit-filled are eager to pray. It is not a sour duty but a glorious pleasure and privilege. Jesus said, "Howbeit when He, the Spirit of truth, is come, He...shall glorify Me" (John 16:13, 14 KJV).

A SIGN OF PENTECOST

When Solomon dedicated the Temple, the light of the *"shekinah,"* the visible glory of God, shone on the golden Mercy Seat in the Holy of Holies. After he prayed, the entire area, the Holy Place and the outside courts, was filled with the glory so that the priests could not enter, and they fell to the floor in worship and thanksgiving (2 Chronicles 7:1-3). That is an Old Testament picture.

FULL HOUSE

If we are saved, the light of Christ dwells in the shrine of our inner hearts, but when we pray for the Holy Spirit, He breaks forth throughout our entire beings: spirit, soul, mind and body. He floods and baptizes our entire personalities.

ASK, SEEK, KNOCK

Finally, ask; that is all. When we are cleansed through the redeeming blood of Jesus, we are children of God. The baptism in the Holy Spirit becomes our birthright. Jesus encourages us especially about that gift: "Ask...seek...knock...For everyone who asks receives, he who seeks finds, and to him who knocks the door will be opened" (Luke 11:9, 10). "Ask in faith, nothing wavering" (James 1:6 KJV).

NO IMPOSTER

What we receive will only be from God. The devil never answers prayers prayed in the name of Jesus. He has no means of tapping our direct line to heaven if we ask the heavenly Father for the Holy Spirit. No foul demon can impersonate the Holy Spirit and come in His disguise. Read Luke 11:11-13 (NIV):

"Which of you fathers, if your son asks for a fish, will give him a snake instead? Or if he asks for an egg, will give him a scorpion? If you then, though you are evil, know how to give good gifts to your children, how much more will your Father in heaven give the Holy Spirit to those who ask Him!"

That is the final answer. We could not have a more explicit assurance.

WHAT YOU MUST DO NOW

Now that you have read this book, you know what the Lord intends to do in your life: baptize you with the Holy Spirit. Remember that JESUS, and JESUS alone, is the Baptizer (John 1:33). And He is with you right now.

If you have received Jesus as your Lord and personal Savior, your sins are forgiven. You have been washed in the blood of the Lamb of God, cleansed of all your sins, so you qualify to receive this glorious gift. You need not even wait for any special church service. Jesus is with you this very moment. Begin to praise His name.

Worship the Lord, praise His name and you will be baptized by Jesus Christ with the Holy Spirit and with fire.

What the early Christians had is as much for you as for anyone else, because Jesus loves you. Remember, Jesus does not need persuading to do this. He did not need persuading to love you, and He loves you enough to baptize you with the Holy Spirit, now...RIGHT NOW.

Let It Happen!

And now, dear Lord Jesus, let happen to me what happened to the 120 disciples when they were filled with the Holy Spirit. As I read in Mark 16:20 (KJV): "And they went forth, and preached everywhere, the Lord working with them, and confirming the word with signs following. Amen." I will not wait, but humbly embrace Your empowerment, direction and correction. Thank you for your anointing. Let my mortal lips preach the eternal Gospel, and my mortal hands build your eternal Kingdom – to the glory of the Father. May all the world be saved. In Jesus' Name.

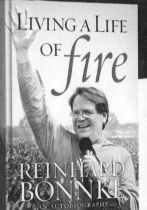

Visit REINHARD BONNKE on Facebook at

Evangelist Reinhard Bonnke - Official Page 🔍

to receive words from the throne of

God daily!

Evangelism is a fiery charlot with a burning messenger, preaching a blazing *Gospel* on wheels of fire!

VISIT US TODAY!